The Restorative School Library

Building Spaces and Programs Where Students Are Seen and Celebrated

Julia Stivers

NEW YORK AND LONDON

Designed cover image: Getty Images

First published 2026
by Routledge
605 Third Avenue, New York, NY 10158

and by Routledge
4 Park Square, Milton Park, Abingdon, Oxon, OX14 4RN

Routledge is an imprint of the Taylor & Francis Group, an informa business

ISBN: 978-1-032-87118-9 (pbk)
ISBN: 978-1-003-56477-5 (ebk)

DOI: 10.4324/9781003564775

Typeset in Palatino
by Newgen Publishing UK

The Restorative School Library

School libraries today are faced with budget cuts, book challenges, "job creep," and more. What is a school librarian to do? Award-winning librarian and ALA author Julia Stivers details how you can navigate these times and build library collections, spaces, and programs where our students are both seen and celebrated.

Stivers shows how restorative practices—including community building, group circles, and actively repairing harm—can work to create more just, equitable spaces where identities and relationships are centered. You'll learn how to build collections that reflect students' identities, lived experiences, and interests, and how to avoid inequitable systems like book fairs, lost book fees, limited check-outs, and biased cataloguing, which create barriers to access for our most vulnerable students.

With the strategies in this book, you'll be able to rethink your procedures, collections, and spaces to make your library restorative for all users.

Julia Stivers (she/her) is a high school librarian in Durham, NC. As an American Library Association Emerging Leader, she helped develop AASL's *Defending Intellectual Freedom: LGBTQ+ Materials in School Libraries*. She is proud to have been named NC's 2022 School Library Media Coordinator of the Year and the 2023 *School Library Journal* School Librarian of the Year. Find her at linktr.ee/BespokeLib.

Equity and Social Justice in Education Series
Paul C. Gorski, Series Editor

Routledge's Equity and Social Justice in Education series is a publishing home for books that apply critical and transformative equity and social justice theories to the work of on-the-ground educators. Books in the series describe meaningful solutions to the racism, white supremacy, economic injustice, sexism, heterosexism, transphobia, ableism, neoliberalism, and other oppressive conditions that pervade schools and school districts.

Creating Inclusive Classrooms for Muslim Students
A Practical Guide for Teachers
Noor Ali

Teaching Environmental Justice in the Elementary Classroom
Entry Points for Equity Across the K-5 Curriculum
Kimi Waite

Ditching Weight Stigma and Anti-Fat Bias at School
Big and Small Equity Fixes for Educators
Cait O'Connor

Social Studies for a Better World
A Guide for Secondary Educators
Delandrea Hall, Katy Swalwell, and Noreen Naseem Rodríguez

Archaeology of Self
The Introspective Educator's Guide to Racial Literacy
Yolanda Sealey-Ruiz

The Restorative School Library
Building Spaces and Programs Where Students Are Seen and Celebrated
Julia Stivers

To my library wives, Kat and Chris.

Your library love—for students, for literature, for advocacy—is a balm.

Contents

Meet the Author

Julia Stivers (she/her)—currently the Upper School Librarian at Carolina Friends School—has worked with teens in many different settings, including school libraries, as a writing facilitator, and through literacy outreach with incarcerated youth. She received her MSLS from the School of Information and Library Science at the University of North Carolina and answers to both Julie and Julia!

Julia's research and practical interests center on inclusive libraries, restorative school spaces, reimagined school book fairs, and exploring the power of manga with her students. Her work has been published in *School Libraries Worldwide*, *Knowledge Quest*, *School Library Journal*, and *YALS*. She is the author/editor of *Include* (ALA, 2022) and the co-author of *Manga Goes to School* (ALA, 2025). As an American Library Association Emerging Leader, Julia helped develop AASL's *Defending Intellectual Freedom: LGBTQ+ Materials in School Libraries*. She's proud to have been named a 2019 *Library Journal* Mover & Shaker, NC's 2022 School Library Media Coordinator of the Year, and the 2023 *School Library Journal* School Librarian of the Year.

Julia is happiest when working directly with students—in the library, classroom, and through clubs. She loves co-presenting with her students at conferences on topics ranging from anime programming and the #LibFive to expanding the role of the library helper and neurodivergent-authored literature. Find her online at linktr.ee/BespokeLib.

Introduction

As librarians, we understand *authority* when evaluating a resource. Does the author have expertise on the resource topic? Are they a subject expert? It feels indulgent to establish the authority of *this* resource—seeing as how I wrote it—but I'm too awkward to ask someone else to establish my credibility for me while I blush off page.

What makes me a credible resource on restorative libraries? On restorative spaces, collections, and programming? I could talk about titles or awards or articles, but I'd rather tell you about Kevin. About Miles. About Jaida and Jonathan and Desi. Angel, Sanai, and Andy. Nia and Owen. Alex, Adrian, Isabella, and Leo. The way that I know best to tell you about my students and how wonderful they are is to talk about the libraries we've transformed together.

I'm going to tell you about those libraries in this book. I'm going to talk about restorative circulation policies, building a soft place to land, and a collection that reflects and engages our students. Microaffirmations, inclusive clubs, and reimagined book fairs. Healing literary practices, reading community, and ditching Dewey. I don't know how to talk about librarianship *without* situating it as *restorative*.

I'm not a consultant, central office employee, or district supervisor. I am a full-time school librarian, and I know how

DOI: 10.4324/9781003564775-1

busy we are. I am not going to waste your time. I'm not going to share an idea or practice unless I've done it and lived it and seen that *it matters*. Building restorative library collections, spaces, and relationships is an aspect of librarianship that is evidenced in my practice—in how I *librarian*. [Yes, we're making *librarian* a verb.] No *one* book is going to cover everything that librarians do. With this book, I'm illustrating concepts and ideas on an aspect of librarianship I'm good at. Believe me, I'm not good at them all! I'm excited to read *your* book about *your* librarian specialty—perhaps on information literacy, collection development policies, or merging STEM and literacy. But practicing unapologetically student-centered librarianship in an equity-grounded space that affirms students? *That's a restorative library.* And it's a subject I *always* want to talk about.

We're going to travel through ten chapters together, beginning with a core restorative concept: keeping students at the center. Then, we'll discover restorative spaces, collections, library policies, and instruction. We'll cover restorative practices—officially—and how they can be incorporated into a school library program. I'll reframe library marketing as seeing and unpack what can make clubs and author visits equitable for our students. I'll share a reimagined book fair model and how we can move our library helpers beyond clerical tasks.

Each chapter will include a *Chapter Roadmap*—for readers who like to know where each chapter trail leads. At the opposite end of each chapter will be questions and reflections to *Leverage Your Expertise*. You each are experts on your own libraries and students! Combining that expertise and experience with the ideas in each chapter can mix and meld into powerful, restorative ideas for your libraries.

1

Students at the Center: The #LibFive

Fresh out of library school, I was excited to begin work at Mount Vernon Middle, a public, alternative school with small class sizes and a goal towards academic *recovery*. The *alternative* in the description meant that our students had not achieved success—as defined by the single metric of grades—at their base schools from across our large county district. I was excited to engage with students who were starting fresh at a new school, and I had dreams and plans for what we could do together in the library.

I faltered when I actually saw the library space. It was… barren. Devoid of color, energy, and most importantly, students. A computer lab with ancient desktop computers took up a third of the limited space, along with an enormous circulation desk. There were outdated posters on the walls, and the shelves were full of books from end to end: about 70% non-fiction and 30% fiction, with one spinning wire shelf of graphic novels and manga. The color palette—driven by the outdated non-fiction spines—was overwhelmingly *brown*. After a quick perusal of the books, however, a different color palette emerged: *white*. Not only were the titles outdated, they were overwhelmingly white, straight, and Christian. I wish I had taken pictures of those first few days to enable a dramatic DIY-reveal, but I was too busy. I started gutting the space and collection that summer.

DOI: 10.4324/9781003564775-2

When the school year started, it became clear that the librarian before me had primarily seen her role as a technology contact for teachers and a "keeper" of the room and books. There was no culture of reading or a history of content collaborations with teachers. The librarian was expected to cover ALC (Alternative Learning Community which here meant ISS) at lunchtime and other scheduled periods—meaning that the library was closed at these times. Frequent district meetings for adults were held in the space, also closing the library for students. The yearly budget for all library spending—including books—was $500.

Why am I beginning a chapter on how to keep students at the center by detailing the realities of my first school library when I started? Let me fast forward to June and provide a snapshot of the library at the end of that first school year.

- Circulation had improved by over 150%.
- The library was open for lunch and full of students each day.
- With content teachers, I had collaborated on lessons varying from 6th-grade Egyptian history to a 7th-grade genetically modified food Socratic Seminar to an 8th-grade literature and augmented reality project.
- I'd advocated for the inclusion of several titles as class texts in ELA classes, including *The Crossover* by Kwame Alexander and *Yummy* by G. Neri.
- There were no more day-long district meetings in our library. The library was closed for *them*, not my students.
- The library had been awarded over $3000 in grant funding for new books.
- I'd weeded over 800 titles from the collection, compared to 32 the previous year. These titles were outdated, inaccurate, and/or in poor condition.
- 986 new books had been added compared to that of 73 the previous year.
- The outdated computer lab was gone, as students had classroom sets of laptops to use.

- The walls were painted.
- Book covers flooded the space.
- I had successfully run our first #TrueBookFAIR.
- I'd advocated for a budget increase for the following year to $5000.
- I no longer covered ALC and was able to have the library open for students during lunch.

The library had been remade. Remade to reflect my students—their identities, lived experiences, and interests. Remade to be a hub of literacy, engagement, and joy in the school. Remade to keep students at the center.

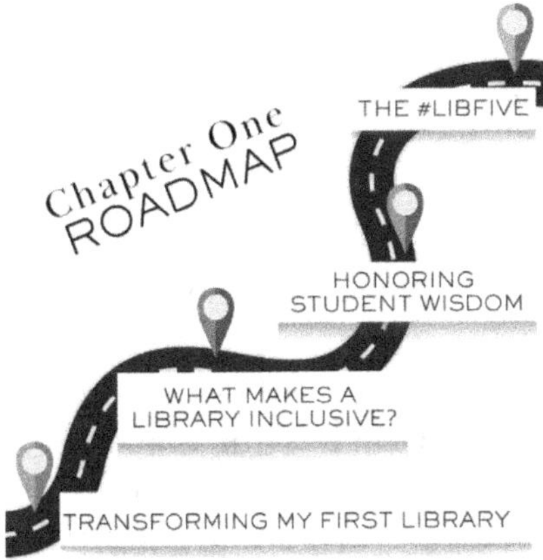

The #LibFive

My student population was unique in that I was welcoming students to my library throughout each year whom had been at multiple schools previous to ours—typically several elementary and middle schools. Our population was overwhelmingly male-identified, over 80%, and overwhelmingly BIPOC, about 90% Black and/or Latinx. As I welcomed a new cohort of students to our library during that next year and beyond, it became clear that my students and I had created something special in our tiny physical space that first year. Time and again, I heard from my students that this was the first library they'd ever willingly returned to and which had inspired them to become frequent library users. The first library that they had been excited to check out a book from. The first library they'd wanted to spend their free time in. This was both powerful and humbling, but it saddened me that my students had not had positive library experiences in other schools.

In the interests of helping other librarians grow their collections and libraries to be more inclusive, I began sharing my strategies with other librarians in my district. My goal was to share experiences to help us all build inclusive libraries where all students—especially our most vulnerable students—were both centered and cherished. I knew, though, what was missing from any professional development or presentation on building inclusive library programs: student testimony, experiences, and wisdom.

Through my studies at UNC-Chapel Hill, I learned about the *Student Six*, a student-led professional development for teachers centering on six culturally sustaining strategies for educators to use to better connect with their BIPOC students.[1] Every time I had seen the teens and their educator, Teresa Bunner, present on the Student Six, a question arose from the audience of mostly librarians or soon-to-be librarians: *What was your experience with school libraries?* The answers were lukewarm at best, and none of the teens in attendance at these PD sessions had meaningful or positive stories to share about their experiences with school librarians. I had always thought that we needed a school library equivalent of the Student Six, as I wanted to hear students talk about culturally sustaining strategies through the specific lens of libraries. After being at Mount Vernon, I thought, *why not us*? Our students had experiences with multiple schools, and they were able to come to Mount Vernon and rewrite their school stories. Part of that rewriting naturally happened in the library.

I looked for student volunteers to thought-partner with me on why our Mount Vernon library was successful, hoping to share usable information with other librarians through student-led PD. I identified an enrichment/remediation period where I could do this work with students several days each week. To honor the students' time and labor devoted to this task during the school day, they received academic credit.[2] Three 8th-grade students, using the pseudonyms Mateo, Hector, and Jayla, spent months together with me at Mount Vernon trying to boil down what made a library inclusive and welcoming to all students. We were thinking primarily in terms of BISOC, because as Mateo would often explain to other librarians when presenting "that's what we are." Before we started looking at their own library experiences, we unpacked key scholarship together including:

- Dr. Kafi Kumasi's research, which found that many students of color felt like outsiders in their libraries and that the library often seemed like it was a place "owned" by the librarian.[3]
- Hanley and Noblit's study, which found that for youth of color, positive racial identity leads to academic success.[4]
- The Cooperative Children's Book Center Diversity Statistics and infographics.
- The strategies of the Student Six: visibility, proximity, connecting to students' lives, engaging students' cultures, addressing race, and connecting to the larger world and students' future selves.

Jayla, Mateo, and Hector then embarked on their own action-based research. They conducted library walks, taking notes on their observations. They thought about the libraries at their former schools and their experiences there, in addition to interviewing classmates about their experiences at other schools and at Mount Vernon. We brainstormed about what makes a library feel welcoming. We initially came up with eleven ideas for what librarians can do to be truly welcoming to all of their students. We spent months on this project, eventually shaping our list into the five ways that libraries can be welcoming and inclusive. We called our list the *#LibFive: Five Key Foundations for Building Inclusive Libraries*. These weren't five ideas to sprinkle onto a library program—they were foundational and, in our eyes, necessary for an equity-based library. Our five foundations were:

- See me! Listen to me.
- Show me on the shelves and walls. Read those books yourself.
- Graphic novels and manga are not extra.
- Show the joy in our stories.
- Make the library a sorting free zone.

We weren't intending for these five ideas to sound revolutionary, and we knew that some would find them to be simple. *Simple does not mean easy*. These foundations are compelling due to their straightforwardness. When we enact these foundations consistently and in powerful ways, they can help us create empowering, student-centered library programs.

1 See Me! Listen To Me

Mateo asked librarians to see their students, to greet them, and to be excited to see them. He shared that at his last school, no one ever smiled at him when he came into the library. *Smile at us. Be happy to see us*. This seems like such a low bar, doesn't it? Learning students' names and pronouncing them correctly is also a part of this foundation. Additionally, my students identified the need to have someone in the school that they could tell things to, that in their classroom, there was often not time. Mateo would simply say: *Ms. Stivers lets us tell her things*.

Jason Reynolds said: Your students don't need you to save them. They need you "to see them."[5] As a white librarian working with primarily Black and Latinx students, this felt particularly necessary to embody. We cannot slip into any kind of a savior role. I am not saving my students by supporting them academically, introducing them to authors who look like them, or listening to their interests. I'm *seeing* them. In addition to seeing our students at the individual level, we can *see* our students at a more macro-level by pushing back against colorblindness and doing our own internal work to push against biases.

2 Show Me on the Shelves and Walls: Read Those Books Yourself

Every student that walks into a library deserves to see themselves reflected in the books on the shelves—reflected in terms of their identities, lived experiences, and interests. If we use the seminal Windows and Mirrors scholarship from Dr. Rudine Sims Bishop[6], all our students need to feel mirrored in a way that affirms who they are. As librarians, we should all know, understand, and believe in this core tenet of librarianship. Being able to explain the value of inclusive literature to stakeholders is paramount, especially amidst the toxic landscape of book banning we're living in. These are the major points I use with stakeholders—whether that is families, administration, colleagues, or a school board—to advocate for inclusive, reflective collections.

- There is inherent value to be gained for all of us from sharing stories that reflect the rich tapestry of human experience.
- Inclusive literature increases student engagement with reading.
- Inclusive literature increases the amount of time students spend reading. Further, reading growth can drive academic growth across all subjects.
- When students see themselves reflected in literature, it builds confidence and a positive self-image.
- Diversifying collections has been shown to increase reading scores.[7]
- Culturally relevant literature can improve critical thinking skills.[8]
- Inclusive literature builds empathy in students.
- From my experiences as a youth librarian, inclusive books literally save lives. My students have told me *I'm still here* because of a specific book or author.

As a white librarian, I typically don't use the term: *diverse* literature. Ironically, I've found that this term can actually end up centering white, Christian, straight, and/or English-speaking narratives as *typical*—or even worse, *regular*—literature and label all other types of literature as *diverse*, something extra. This is essentially *othering* stories that don't fall into a narrow category of books written by groups holding places of power. I use the term *reflective*—of our school populations and/or the global majority—or my preferred term, *inclusive*. Key to our understanding of literature is that by centering marginalized stories and communities, we are opening up our libraries to the full slate of available great stories. Inclusive literature is not a category of books that are extraneous or something to add to our collections. They *are* our collections.

The second part of this key foundation—read those books yourself—is a necessary reality for librarians. Our own reading habits need to reflect our inclusive collections and reflect what our students are interested in. Jayla would remind librarians that she didn't just want libraries to have the books we were promoting in our presentations; she wanted librarians to be able to talk to their students about these beautiful books. Jayla would share with other librarians: *I can see myself all over the books in my Mount Vernon library and I can talk with Ms. Stivers about them.*

3 Graphic Novels and Manga Are Not Extra

When we would present on the #LibFive, Hector would always choose this foundation to talk about. His love for *Dog Man* by Dav Pilkey was boundless and infectious, and it was the perfect jumpstart into why graphic novels—including manga—are so vital to equitable libraries. It seems unimaginable that today, stakeholders are still questioning the value of graphic novels in schools, but they *are*. Additionally, because of graphic novels' visual brand of storytelling, they are particularly vulnerable to censorship and book bans. Similar to inclusive literature, I've found it helpful to be extremely familiar with key talking points to use with anyone questioning the value of graphic novels. Having this kind of evidence at the ready is crucial to safeguarding the presence of graphic novels in our schools.

- Research has shown that students who read graphic novels in their free time are "twice as likely to enjoy reading overall and are much more likely to rate themselves as good readers as compared to those who do not read graphic novels."[9]
- Graphic novels have complex vocabulary: up to 20% more complex than books with only text.[10]
- Graphic novels can improve students' reading skills, including scoring higher on comprehension tests.[11]
- Exposing students to different formats can both aid emerging readers and challenge adept readers.
- Graphic novels enhance critical thinking skills as they require readers to integrate textual and visual literacy. Readers interpret images and words, identify and understand visual cues, and analyze panel sequences. Comfort with multimodal literacy is crucial for students who are decoding digital information on a consistent basis.

Flooding our libraries with graphic novels not only offers substantial literacy benefits, but engagement and circulation will also increase in our spaces. Each year, more graphic novels are being published that not only engage our readers, but connect to the curriculum and courses of study. To truly advocate for graphic novels, we also have to work to embed them in classes. Collaborating with teachers in our schools is a powerful way to support both our students' literacy and their interests. Using a graphic novel for a co-taught or librarian-led lesson models to our colleagues that graphic novels are literature—worthy of study in the classroom—from elementary to high school.

Collaborating with teachers can be challenging due to both the time investment necessary and the need for constant advocacy work to "sell" ourselves as literacy leaders—especially as some of us are being tasked with more and more chromebook deployment and device management. The rewards, though, are many: increased classroom time with students, opportunities to promote library resources, and knowing that we're infusing the curriculum with engaging texts that our students want to read. Adding graphic novels to our repertoire of possible content collaborations can boost not only the transformative power of collaboration, but will help solidify our role as literacy experts in our schools.

Manga—or comics originating in Japan—have a unique place in a restorative library. The popularity of manga amongst youth around the world continues to grow, including in our schools. In our library guide, *Manga Goes to School* (ALA, 2025), my co-authors and I clearly situate manga as being a necessary part of equitable library spaces as there is a connection between manga and marginalized communities. Certainly, no community is a monolith—our students have unique interests and lived experiences within identity groups. As working librarians, however, we had all noticed that many of our manga readers are members of one or more communities—such as BISOC, Queer, and Neurodivergent. As more research and attention continues to be devoted to the over-represented manga readership of marginalized communities, we can ensure we're serving our students by devoting both time and resources into collecting this powerful format. After all, when we celebrate manga—and graphic novels as a whole—we are also celebrating their readers!

4 Show the Joy in Our Stories

When my students were doing their action-based research as part of our #LibFive creation, the first thing Jayla wrote down while walking around our Mount Vernon Library was "Black people look good." I thought I understood what she meant, but I asked her to unpack her thinking behind the observation. Jayla shared that when she walked around our library, she saw cover art on titles where Black characters were centered as romantic leads, fantasy main characters (MCs), and action heroines. In her previous libraries, Jayla had been used to seeing Black characters on covers only as part of civil rights narratives or biographies. Jayla shared that when she saw the beauty and futures of Black characters on book covers, she was seeing the beauty of and possible futures for herself.

Jayla talked about the importance of joy in literature using Black narratives because that is her lived experience lens. We were not suggesting that books that deal with real history—including the horror and tragedy of enslavement and Jim Crow—should not be included in our libraries. Of course, real history is vital to our collections—both in terms of non-fiction and historical fiction, taking special care to foreground titles written by Black authors. Stories of pain and overcoming trauma cannot be the only examples where Black stories take center stage, however. Every genre and sub-genre in our libraries needs to center narratives where Black MCs are living—wielding magic, solving crimes, crushing on their best friend, traveling through space—and living intersectionally, as, for example, disabled, trans, Muslim, and/or with ADHD. Audre Lorde said that we don't live "single-issue lives."[12] Our students don't either, and that means our book characters also cannot!

In "Don't Just Read About Racism—Read Stories About Black People Living," author Nic Stone explains why all of the anti-racist reading lists that popped up in the summer of 2020 aren't enough. She stressed the necessity of Black stories showing the wealth of human experience and possibilities. She shared about her reading history as a child:

> As far as I knew then, Black girls like me didn't *exist* in books. And as physics would have it, people who don't *exist* can't go on adventures or solve mysteries or fall in love or save the universe. Which meant that I, as a non-existent entity, wasn't capable of any of those things. And I wasn't the only person getting this message. Anyone reading books without me in them was getting it too.
>
> (Stone, 2020)

Again, I'm using Black narratives as an example because that is the lived experience lens that Jayla was an expert on, but this framework is true for every marginalized community. Author Malinda Lo said it beautifully when she said that, of course, we need books that talk about race and racism, but "we also need books where characters of color can simply have the same kind of plot-driven adventures that white characters have all the time."[13] (*Chapter 3: Curating a Restorative Collection* has more on this framing.) Malindo Lo's powerful statement has influenced my collection development strategies since my first year as a librarian, and it is clearly echoed by *Show the Joy in Our Stories*.

5 Make the Library a Sorting-Free Zone

Our students get sorted into categories all day at school—intentionally or unintentionally—by a multitude of factors, including academic grades, perceived behavior, gender, and test scores. One of the reasons that libraries can be such sanctuaries is that they can be—*should be*—spaces where our students do *not* get sorted. After all, we are one of the few school spaces where academic grades do not typically get assessed. Lean into this reality by believing that every visitor (which should be every student) is automatically an A+ library user. In the library, our expectation should be that every student *is* successful and *will be* successful. This also goes for any perceived behavior issues that colleagues may share with you about a student or any struggles you've witnessed in classrooms or the cafeteria. As equity-minded educators, we must be aware that many perceived behavior issues are rooted in racial bias. Every step into the library is a fresh start, for both the student and their interactions with you.

In terms of perceived gender, an easy fix to make to our language is to simply de-gender it. There is no reason to say boys and girls or ladies and gentlemen. By doing this, we're automatically othering our gender nonconforming students. Use collective nouns like students, readers, or folks—whatever fits your school culture and your own vibe. As a librarian in North Carolina, I usually reach for the all-encompassing *y'all*.

There is another way our students get sorted in our school libraries. A situation which literally causes them to pay money for resources and even access to our spaces. What makes these events so egregious is that our school libraries should always center equitable access to resources. Paul Gorski found that for economically disadvantaged parents, these events formed their "most embarrassing" school experiences.[14] What often beloved library event am I referring to? Traditional school book fairs. The traditional school book fair model turns our libraries into for-profit satellite shops for publishers, forcing students and families into paying for books to take home from our libraries. Students are automatically sorted into those who can pay (or remember to bring) money to purchase books and those who cannot. This kind of book "fair" does not align with its name.

Some of the goals for book fairs are positive, as they can generate excitement for reading, build connections with teachers, and offer a pathway to more books in the home. If we reimagine the traditional book fair, we can still champion reading for pleasure while preventing inequitable sorting based on family finances. At Mount Vernon, I created a different kind of fair, where students selected new books to keep from a bespoke fair collection that I had intentionally curated to reflect both our students and their interests. There was never any cost to students. *(Read more about the logistics of #TrueBookFAIRs—including ideas for finding funding to run your own—in Chapter 9.)*

LEVERAGE YOUR EXPERTISE

- What are some ways you have already transformed your library? What new areas or programs in your library are now ready to be transformed?
- Which foundation(s) in the #LibFive is(are) already a strength for your library program?
  - See me. Listen to me.
  - Show me on the shelves and walls. Read those books yourself.
  - Graphic novels and manga are not extra.
  - Show the JOY in our stories.
  - Make the library a sorting-free zone.
- Which foundation represents a meaningful growth opportunity you'd like to focus on? How can you enlist student feedback to grow this area of your library program? For example, if you chose number four—Graphic Novels and Manga are not extra—you could:

- Assemble a team of students who are graphic novel superfans—including readers of manga! This team can offer purchasing suggestions of titles and series, create displays, and even redesign your graphic novel shelving.
- Identify grant opportunities you could apply for with your students to find funding for all the new titles you'll be purchasing!
- Identify a class where you could collaborate and advocate for the inclusion of a graphic novel as a class text. Social studies and history classes frequently provide opportunities for rich curriculum connections with a graphic text.

The #LibFive Continues

It has been almost ten years since Hector, Mateo, Jayla, and I created the #LibFive. Those five deceptively simple foundations still ring true for me today, even at a completely different school. *See Me! Listen to me. Show me on the shelves and walls. Read those books yourself. Graphic novels and manga are not extra. Show the joy in our stories. Make the library a sorting free zone.* We can all walk into our school libraries every day, ready to live out these five key foundations to always, always keep students at the center.

Notes

1 Bunner, T. (2017). When We Listen: Using student voices to design culturally responsive and just schools. *Knowledge Quest*, 3(45), 39–45.

2 As a result of their work being included in Project READY (https://ready.web.unc.edu/), my students were also financially compensated for their time.

3 Kumasi, K. (2012). Roses in the concrete: A critical race perspective on urban youth and school libraries. *Knowledge Quest, 40*(5), 31–3.

4 Hanley, M. and Noblit, G. W. (2009). *Cultural responsiveness, racial identity and academic success: a review of literature*. Prepared for The Heinz Endowments.

5 Krok, Lisa. 2018. "ALSC Charlemae Rollins President's Program." *American Libraries* (June 26) (accessed March 23, 2023).

6 Bishop, R. S. (1990). Mirrors, windows, and sliding glass doors. *Perspectives: Choosing and Using Books for the Classroom*, 6(3).

7 First Book. (2023). The Impact of a Diverse Classroom Library. Washington, DC: First Book.

8 Christ, T. (2018). Cultural relevance and informal reading inventory performance: African-American primary and middle school students. *Literacy Research and Instruction*, 57(2), 117–134.

9 Clark, C., Starbuck Graidley, L., Cole, A., and Chamberlain, E. (2024). *Children and Young People's Engagement with Comics in 2023*. National Literacy Trust.

10 Gavigan, K.W. and Tomasevich, M. (2011). *Connecting comics to curriculum: Strategies for grades 6–12*. Santa Barbara, CA: Libraries Unlimited.

11 Aldahash, R. and Sultan Altalhab, S. (2020). The Effect of Graphic Novels on EFL Learners' Reading Comprehension. *International Journal of Applied Linguistics and English Literature*, 9(5), 19–26.

12 Lorde, A. (1982). *Learning from the 60s*. Speech delivered at Harvard for Black History Month. Cambridge, MA.

13 Lo, M. (2015). *Recommended Read: The Third Twin by CJ Omololu*. Malinda Lo Blog, February 24, 2015.

14 Gorski, P. (2022). Stop Punishing Poverty in Schools. *ASCD Educational Leadership*, 80(4), 22–28

2

Building a Restorative Space

Our students take a lot of steps—both literally and figuratively—each day in our schools. I would like the step students take into our library spaces to be the easiest step they make all day. Stepping into a place where they can both bring their full selves and carve out their own space in a shared community. To build these kinds of physical library spaces, I lean on two tenets of restorative practices: co-creating a sense of belonging and repairing harm. We can do this in our libraries in a multitude of logistical and thematic ways, including through micro-affirmations, displays and signage, and comfort and accessibility.

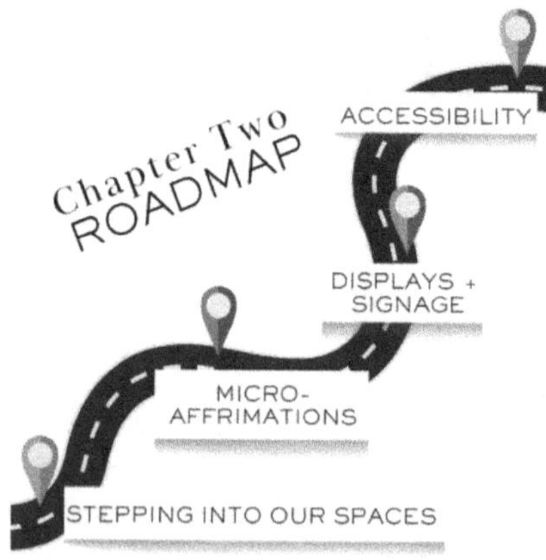

DOI: 10.4324/9781003564775-3

Micro-Affirmations

Many of our students encounter microaggressions throughout their school days. They may be bombarded with verbal, behavioral, and environmental slights that communicate and reinforce racist, heterosexist, and sexist attitudes and biases. As educators, part of our jobs is making sure that we are working to minimize any microaggressive behavior from our own interactions and pedagogy, including how to respond effectively when we've committed one. It is not enough, however, to simply minimize or remove microaggressions. A thread running through this chapter—and book—is that there is no neutrality when it comes to equity-focused librarianship. We have to actively seek to repair harm, always. Towards this end, making micro*affirmations* a part of each day is a key tenet of a restorative library.

Microaffirmations are the small signals that welcome, invite, and celebrate our students, including their identities, lived experiences, and interests. Microaffirmations are authentic ways we can work to negate the harm our students experience each day. What can this look like? Quick examples include:

- Knowing many of my students' favorite trans author—Andrew Joseph White—and ensuring that I have posters of his books front and center.
- Knowing the necessity of fidgets for my neurodivergent students and always having them on hand—easily accessible, so they don't need to ask for them.
- Featuring a Black Lives Matter flag in concert with a library full of Black-authored books.

Naturally, only offering microaffirmations in a larger context of institutionalized inequity is ***meaningless***. If I smile at a student who still might feel invisible based on the displayed books, it is not equitable or restorative. We need more than high-optic, low-impact options that are just surface-level. And, we still *do need* the high-optic options—in concert with sustainable, high-impact change. A library that provides microaffirmations is a highly visible clue that the space is invested in meaningful change and advocacy.

Microaffirmations must include true visibility. We can't affirm what we don't see. Our students should feel visible and seen in the space. This is easier to achieve when we co-create our spaces together with our students. A sense of ownership will naturally follow when students feel empowered to enact change, make suggestions, and are invited to make decisions that impact the library. Also, do not underestimate the power of a smile! Co-creator of the #LibFive, Mateo's main complaint about past libraries was that *no one smiled at him when he came into the library.* A warm, welcoming smile for every student is essential.

We can embed microaffirmations into our spaces through intentional displays. As our students from marginalized communities—including trans students, students born in another country, Queer students, and/or BIPOC students—continue to see hurtful propaganda, policies, and legislation on a local, state, and/or national level, we can build visual counter stories. Some examples of different displays I've created to directly respond to outside events:

- In 2017, after the white nationalist "Unite the Right" rally in Charlottesville, and the president at that time said there were "some very fine people" on both sides, I created a permanent display called: *This Library Takes Side*s. It was filled with rotating books written by BIPOC authors and quotes from Black leaders.
- In 2018, after the then-President enacted biased travel bans on citizens from six predominantly Muslim countries, a permanent wall display went above the library door that said: *In this library, students of all religions and countries of origin are welcomed and celebrated.* Picture book *Dreamers* by Yuyi Morales and covers of MG and YA books written by authors representing a wide range of religions and countries of origin were featured.
- In 2021, after our then NC Lieutenant Governor made public, hateful statements about the LGBTQ+ community, the next day, the library had a bookcase claiming

Pride is Beautiful filled with books written by LGBTQ+ authors.

- Vile comments made at a presidential rally in 2024 about Puerto Rico? You guessed it. I created a wall display filled with beautiful images of the Puerto Rican landscape and covers of books written by Puerto Rican authors.
- After January 20, 2025, when harmful executive orders began to proliferate, I created a side-by-side wall display featuring book covers and signs for *Books Celebrating Trans and Non-Binary Authors* and *Books Featuring Teens Overthrowing Oppressive Governments.*
- In April 2025, when a government official made false and horrific claims about Autistic people, I made a display of *Award Winning Books Written by Autistic Authors.*

Do I think these displays undo the very real harm being done? *Of course not.* When they are enacted in the context of an antiracist, anti-heterosexist culture I'm trying to build, they do signal to our students, however, both what their library values and how much their library values *them.* Research has shown that for LGBTQ+ students, having just one supportive educator can help mitigate harm.[1] With these kinds of displays, we can build a supportive space.

Displays and Signage

Microaffirmations are just one way to think of displays and signage in a restorative library. No matter how we create thematic displays, content is always paramount to style. Our displays don't have to be Pinterest-worthy; they just need to be powerful. Honestly, my bulletin-board or wall displays are simple. They center on a common idea and feature clear images of book covers in a collage. My go-to wall displays might sound basic:

- Adaptations (combining the literary source material with currently popular or about-to-be-released series, movies, games, and anime)

- Summer or Winter Reads.
- Collaborations, for example, Mental Health Awareness with our counselor, Neurodiversity with our Learning Specialist, and Cool Science with a science teacher.
- School Activities, which connect a school event, such as a play, concert, or playoff game, with a display of titles.
- Monthly celebrations where I'm clear that inclusive books are not limited to days on a calendar. For example: *We Can Celebrate Black History-Genius-Power-Excellence All Year Through Literature* or *Read Great Books by Asian-American Authors All Year*.

A more complicated, permanent wall display in our library is a Historical Fiction Timeline. The idea came from Tom Bober, an elementary librarian in Missouri. In addition to historical fiction—both text-only and graphic novels—I include narrative nonfiction and nonfiction graphic novels in a visual, linear arrangement broken out by time–centuries and decades. This not only makes the historical fiction collection more browsable, but it also helps with history collaborations and readers' advisory.

My favorite constantly changing bookshelf display is, again, simple. As we juggle hundreds of tasks a day, I've found that easily sustainable display ideas help make our spaces both engaging and accessible. In a highly visible spot, I have a rotating display with colorful signage that says: "Read Colorfully. New Hues Each Month." On this display, I or my student helpers choose a different color each month, and we flood that shelf with outward-facing titles across genres and formats that all have a shared cover color. Red, purple, pink, blue, yellow—whatever you and your students choose. This works for all age ranges and is a great task for library helpers. It is not only a beautiful display, but a popular one. Students are always grabbing books from this display, and it's easy to restock. No catalog search necessary—just a quick trip around the library to find more books with the right color cover.

I keep using the word *simple*, because I want to spend time collecting books to reflect the tapestries that are my students, not on creating elaborate art projects in the library that highlight my craft skills. The key is the actual content—and chosen books—of all of these wall or shelf displays. They should be microcosms of our inclusive library collections. Whether it's a shelf display of orange covers or a blue and white maelstrom of winter reads on a wall display, ensure that each includes a wide range of identities representing the diversity of human experience. Additionally, graphic novels and manga should always be included, again, no matter the theme of the display. If it's not possible to build each display with deep intersectional representation and multiple formats, it is a growth opportunity for your collection. *(See Chapter 3: Curating a Restorative Collection for more information.)*

Signage in our libraries is another opportunity to build a restorative space. Choose signage that welcomes students, broadcasts your library's values, spreads joy, and fosters belonging. Signage suggestions for a restorative library:

- *Book cover posters*. Enlarge your beautiful, inclusive book covers to 11 by 17 size at an office supply store and then laminate the copies. Voilà! Instant posters. Not only do these posters beautify the space and affirm your students, but they also advertise your collection and serve as passive readers' advisory.
- *READ posters with student images*. Based on the library-iconic posters of celebrities created by the American Library Association, build your own with images of your own students (with permission, of course) holding self-selected library titles. These posters should accurately reflect your student population.
- *Art dedicated to social justice*. Amplifier (amplifer.org) has over 1000 artworks available for free, non-commercial download. Choose posters with your students from a variety of social justice lenses to print and display in your space.

- *Student artwork*. You can include student artifacts from your art collaborations or invite students to create permanent murals in your space.
- *Specific signs that telegraph your experiences, training, and values*. Are you safe zone trained? Advertise that. Any signage that telegraphs who we are and how we are going to show up for and with our students can be a welcome addition.
- *Your library's story*. I don't create a narrative end-of-year report. Instead, I create student-centered, image-dominated infographics. Visit mtvernonlibrary.weebly.com/a-look-back to see examples of posters I've created in the past. This is an opportunity to visually represent your library values by showing students joyfully reading—and thriving—in your space. Additionally, it will give you and your students ownership of your library's story, allowing you to highlight what you've created together, learned together, and celebrated together.
- *Norms instead of rules*. The word *no* does not appear anywhere in our library space. Neither does the word *rules*. In my experience, rules are just something to be broken, whereas norms or community agreements are something we can build together.
- *Recognizing the impact of library vocabulary*. Hi-Lo books is a term which publishers use to refer to short books with a high interest level, but a low reading level. For example, it may be a book about a whirlwind high school romance with disapproving parents, but written at a 4th-grade reading level. These books definitely have a place in inclusive libraries, but I never refer to them as hi-lo books and would never use signage to refer to them this way. I've seen Hi-Lo Book signage in other libraries—please do not do this! The word "low" should never be used to publicly describe a students' reading level. I call them Super Short and Suspenseful books available to anybody. The low page number and thin nature of these books will naturally connect them to their readers without advertising them as Hi-Lo.
- *Intentionality with every sign*. When I came to my current library, there was a sign for books in Spanish that had

> the words *Libros en Español* on top of the Spanish flag. At first glance, that might seem innocuous, but do most of our Spanish-speaking students in our schools come from Spain? Certainly not. Why should we represent the language of so many of our families by using a colonizer's flag? Instead, I changed the sign to contain the flags of where the majority of my Latinx students had ancestry from: the Dominican Republic, Mexico, Puerto Rico, and Honduras. It's a tiny shift in thinking on one small sign, but every choice we make in our libraries adds up to a large impact for our students.

We have to *live* our signs. If it hangs on our walls, it needs to hang on our pedagogy as a trait we authentically inhabit.

Depending on the freedom afforded to you as an educator in your school context, you may not always feel empowered to display signs that fully embrace your values. I realize that I am sharing my experiences from a place of privilege as a white, cis educator, and I am not suggesting you hang a sign that is going to cause you to lose your job. I am suggesting, however, that we have to figure out a way—in all of our school contexts—to celebrate and protect our students. I have worked with both progressive and conservative administrations and have found success with both by leaning into literacy, visibility, and joy.

Obviously, you understand your school context better than I do! As I'm writing this book, we are experiencing a sustained, vile attack on schools and freedom, which necessitates us as equity-focused librarians to be strategic. Paul Gorski and Katy Swallwell address this difficulty in *Fix Injustice, Not Kids*.

> Perhaps there is a time when morality requires some equity-committed leaders to take their stand, to be vulnerable to whatever repercussions may come. Of course, some of us are not in a position to do that, and that has to be OK too. Each of us must decide our best, most principled course of action. We need people to stay in the struggle even in places where the struggle feels at least temporarily fruitless. But we also don't want every equity

> leader to be chased out of schools and districts until there are no adults left who are willing to struggle for equity.[2]

Connect with like-minded equity co-conspirators in your school, district, union or state librarian organization for support as you navigate how best to support students and your equity values amidst any backlash in your school or district.

Comfort and Accessibility

The most student-centered and affirming spaces won't be truly restorative if our students—all of our students—cannot access them. Each of our libraries serves students with disabilities—both visible and less visible. Making our physical spaces accessible is a constant step to co-creating an inclusive space. Some thoughts to consider as we examine our spaces. Thank you to Librarian Ness Shortley who has helped shape my understanding of accessibility needs in library spaces.

- Can a wheelchair user or disabled student using mobility aids such as a cane or crutches navigate the library safely? Is there enough room between shelves, desks, and furniture?
- Are there any tripping hazards such as power cables, unsecured rugs, or low-profile stools that might impede a visually impaired student?
- Is there seating that accommodates all different kinds of bodies?
- Is the check-out computer accessible for all different heights, including someone seated in a wheelchair?
- Is your space neurodivergent friendly? Are there spaces with different noise levels available? Are there finger toys or calming fidgets available for students to access when reading or learning?
- In terms of digital spaces, are there options for students who need accommodations for reading—including digital audiobooks or large print books?

Routine accessibility walks through our spaces can help us identify any barriers to usage for students with different needs. Including students in any library "management" activity is helpful, but use care not to single out or expect labor from disabled students to help you with this task. When we look for accessibility partners, we can reach out to all of our students to allow for self-selection.

Creating a comfortable environment for our students also helps foster a sense of belonging. After all, who wants to truly belong in a space where they are not physically comfortable? Some student-vetted ways to bring comfort to our libraries:

- Beanbags and floor pillows.
- Flexible seating so students can reconfigure the space.
- Blankets and stuffed animals (yes, for high school too).
- Soft lighting.
- Plants.

I've seen repeatedly that *comfort can build courage*. When students feel truly comfortable in our spaces, it will be easier for them to find the bravery to be their full selves.

LEVERAGE YOUR EXPERTISE

- What displays have you built to counter false narratives about our students? What new displays could you build?
- Who in your school, district, or state can you count on as an equity co-conspirator?
- What are the signs in your library communicating to students? Do a walkthrough of your library space(s) with "fresh" eyes. Invite students to do this walk with you. What do you see or notice?
- In what ways could your library program improve its accessibility for all students?

A Soft Place to Land

I've been lucky enough to transform two libraries into restorative spaces using the ideas and frameworks outlined in this chapter. Even though the age ranges, school contexts, and physical spaces were wildly different, the tools to build healing library environments were and are the same. When our overarching goal as school librarians is to both prevent and repair harm in and through our spaces, we can ensure that we are providing our students a soft place to land.

Notes

1 Kosciw, J. G., Clark, C. M., & Menard, L. (2022). *The 2021 National School Climate Survey: The experiences of LGBTQ+ youth in our nation's schools*. New York: GLSEN.
2 Gorski, P. and Swalwell, K. (2023). *Fix Injustice, Not Kids and Other Principles for Transformative Equity Leadership*. ASCD, Arlington, VA.

3

Curating a Restorative Collection

Building a restorative library collection goes beyond the books on our shelves. Collecting books that reflect our students, their identities, and their lived experiences is a crucial baseline for our restorative libraries, but it is just that: a foundation. Building library collections that are restorative also includes weeding responsibly, guarding against soft censorship, and healing reading trauma.

DOI: 10.4324/9781003564775-4

Reflective Collections

To build collections that reflect our students, their lived experiences, and their interests, it's helpful to use a variety of lenses and frameworks. No one list, review source, or idea is going to be enough to build and sustain an inclusive collection. Instead, *diversify* your collection strategies.

Windows, Mirrors, and Sliding Glass Doors

Every reader deserves to see themselves mirrored in the stories they read. The seminal scholarship from Dr. Rudine Sims Bishop[1] is a foundational framework for collecting literature. Conversely, when readers enter a story featuring a character that has a different identity, background, or perspective, it allows the reader to look through a window into other experiences. That window can even turn into a sliding glass door, allowing the reader to step through and engage with the story in a transformative way. Dr. Sims Bishop's essay and metaphor has become so ubiquitous that you may hear colleagues refer to windows and mirrors, without referencing the creator of that analogy. It's an excellent way to model restorative spaces by ensuring that the scholarship of a Black woman is credited. Always, always mention Dr. Rudine Sims Bishop by name. Additionally, ensure that your collection is balanced for your students and that it allows for a plethora of mirrors to affirm who they are.

The Danger of a Single Story

In her influential TED talk, Chimamanda Adichie shares what makes a single story—told about a community—so dangerous.[2] Adichie's TED Talk can be a powerful tool to share with stakeholders who do not fully understand the importance of inclusive literature. As librarians, we *know* the danger of a single story, but Adichie's words can still provide a vital warning for us as we collect titles and search out new stories. Adichie says, "Power is the ability not just to tell the story of another person, but to make it the definitive story of that person." When we are not careful in widely selecting titles, we could end up with a single story of a community in our libraries becoming *the* definitive, harmful story of that community, which all of our students encounter.

For example, a popular text I've used with multiple grades in middle school ELA classrooms is *Yummy: The Last Days of a Southside Shorty* (G. Neri, 2010). This graphic novel based on a true story recounts the tragedies surrounding an 11-year old gang member amidst a series of murders in Chicago in 1994. If that was the only class text I used with a young Black protagonist, I'd be promoting a story that Black youth have sad, violent childhoods like Yummy's in communities where everyone is financially struggling. This is an unbelievably dangerous single story to tell about a community. If we read *Yummy*, I would make sure to also choose a class text like *The Crossover* (K. Alexander, 2014), where the young Black male protagonist comes from an upper-middle-class family and has a stable childhood.

In our libraries, we hold the immense power of selecting books that ultimately tell the story of different communities. When we collect too narrowly, we are flattening the fullness of communities, families, and people. For example, if most of our books written by Latinx authors center on immigration, that becomes the single story of Latinx youth in our spaces. We have to offer so many differing stories that a single story about any community does not exist in our collection. As Adichie reminds us: "The consequence of the single story is this: It robs people of dignity. It makes our recognition of our equal humanity difficult. Stories matter. Many stories matter." Adichie uses words like empower, humanize, and repair in relation to telling limitless stories about peoples and communities. Empower. Humanize. Repair. All tenets of a restorative library and all necessary words to keep in mind when collecting books for our libraries!

Plot-Driven Adventures Across Identities

Author Malinda Lo has referred to the importance of what she called "casual diversity." Lo said that, of course, we need books that talk about race and racism, and "we also need books where characters of color can simply have the same kind of plot-driven adventures that white characters have all the time" (Lo,

2015).[3] I read this statement in my first year as a librarian, and this framework has honestly driven my collection habits perhaps more than any other. *Plot-driven adventures.* This lens works for a wide range of inclusivity. While, of course, we need books where Queer characters come out, we also need books where Queer characters are solving a mystery or saving the world. While, of course, we need books that center issues of immigration justice, we also need books where Latinx characters are discovering secret powers and falling in love. While, of course, we need books where disabled characters are getting the school accommodations they need, we also need books where disabled characters are navigating crushes and traveling in space.

Diversity = Truth

Author Daniel José Older has said when asked about the idea of diversity in books: "I'm fighting for honest books."[4] Reframing our goal in collecting to *honestly represent* the mosaic of human experience is powerful. Again, "diverse books" is not a section in the library—it *is* our library. All students deserve the truth. All students deserve great stories. If we're not including a wide selection of authors representing the fullness of human experience, we're not providing students with all of the great stories available to them.

A Rallying Cry

Django Paris said, "Think of your syllabus as an act of resistance; something to be posted in the streets, handed out at rallies."[5] This is how we can think of our order lists—as an act of resistance. Is my order list tangibly resisting the vile things being said about our Queer students by featuring novels written by Queer authors? Is my order list resisting the movement to block real narratives and erase both the history and current realities of our BIPOC students by overwhelmingly including books written by BIPOC authors? Before I finalize any order, I think of this call, this quote. *Am I proud of my order? Is it a quiet, but powerful rallying cry?*

Looking Beyond Fiction

If we're only spending time to make sure our fiction collections are reflective, we're doing a disservice to our students. We're damaging our readers on two fronts. One, many students prefer non-fiction texts to fiction texts, and the same care must be given in providing books that are reflective for our non-fiction readers. Two, think of the messaging sent to *all* students if the books teaching about history, science, government, and philosophy are written by only white, cishet authors. It's privileging one worldview and background as essential, establishing one kind of author and subject matter as worthy of study. What can this look like in practice? For example, if we just look at the animal world—popular across grade levels—we can build a more inclusive collection by collecting titles such as these by writers from marginalized communities penning books about animals and the natural world.

- **Picture and Board Books**. *Biindigen! Anik Says Welcome* (Nancy Cooper and Joshua Mangeshig Pawis-Steckley, 2023); *Love in the Wild* (Katy Tanis, 2021); *Love Under the Stars* (Katy Tanis, 2024); *Mother of Sharks* (Melissa Cristina Márquez and Devin Elle Kurtz, 2023); *Thanks to the Animals* (Allen Sockabasin and Rebekah Raye, 2014); *The Vast Wonder of the World* (Mélina Mangal and Luisa Urib, 2018).
- **Middle Grade Books and Young Adult Books**. *An Immense World (Young Readers Edition): How Animals Sense Earth's Amazing Secrets* (Ed Yong, 2025); *Queer Ducks (and Other Animals): The Natural World of Animal Sexuality* (Eliot Schrefer, 2022); *Wildlife Anatomy: The Curious Lives & Features of Wild Animals around the World* (Julia Rothman, 2023).
- **Adult Books** (that I have in my high school). *An Immense World: How Animal Senses Reveal the Hidden Realms Around Us* (Ed Yong, 2023); *The Backyard Bird Chronicles* (Amy Tan, 2024); *Beasts of Burden: Animal and Disability Liberation*

(Sunaura Taylor, 2017); *Better Living Through Birding: Notes from a Black Man in the Natural World* (Christian Cooper, 2023); *Evolution's Rainbow: Diversity, Gender, and Sexuality in Nature and People* (Joan Roughgarden, 2013); *How Far the Light Reaches: A Life in Ten Sea Creatures* (Sabrina Imbler, 2024).

Weeding Responsibly

Weeding is a vital step to continually refresh the browsability and usefulness of our collections, our *gardens* of books. To be clear, weeding does not include removing books due to outside pressures that have nothing to do with the suitability of the book for our collection. We weed responsibly when we remove books that are damaged, outdated, contain inaccurate information, or are no longer popular for our students, as indicated by circulation reports/statistics. A school library is not an archive. Our collections need to be updated, accurate, and connect to our current students, their interests, and/or curricular content.

Before my first year as a school librarian, I started weeding my new-to-me collection that summer. It became obvious that the collection had never been weeded. I was ruthless. I found books from the 1950s, books with inaccurate information, and books with clear cultural biases. I threw them all away, recycling where possible. For any books I was unsure about, for example, if it was a reference book that might be used by a teacher, I moved them into an overflow space in the back office. After engaging with teachers for a year, I'd then remove all those books unless they were used for a class. I was just as brutal with the fiction section, but again saved any books I was unsure about into an overflow section. Some of the shelves were now, literally, empty. I was okay with this scenario! I knew that five books on display that my students would want to read were better than 50 aligned in a row; they wouldn't.

There is at times resistance to weeding a library collection. We may feel attached to certain books or remember fondly the motivations we had for purchasing them. It can be helpful to collaborate with a librarian colleague to help you weed if you find yourself struggling. This way, you can each give fresh eyes to your collection and help identify books that need to go. I still use the "purgatory" method and will occasionally remove a book from the shelves, but keep it in another admin area. If a year has gone by and no one has wanted or searched for the book, it'll be an indication that it can be removed permanently.

In your assessment of your collection, you may come across a book that has not been checked out recently (or ever), but that you know is an important book for your restorative library. Perhaps it is a counter-story for a historical event or an award-winning fiction book that has intersectional representation. These books should be kept, no matter the circulation statistics. Through displays, book talks, readers' advisory, or teacher collaborations, you can focus on matching these books to their potential readers.

Guarding Against Soft Censorship

Soft censorship—or self-censorship—is when a librarian removes a book from their collection because of perceived problems or fear about representation in a title. To be clear, soft censorship is not responsible collection development. If, as a middle school librarian, I do not collect a popular fiction book that trusted review sources rate as 9th grade and above, that is not soft censorship. It is simply responsible collection development. If, however, as a middle school librarian, I did not collect, for example, *Heartstopper* (Alice Oseman, 2019)—a hugely popular boy/boy graphic novel romance which is widely reviewed as 7th or 8th grade and above—because I was nervous about Queer content, that *would* be soft censorship.

It is completely understandable to sometimes *think* about outside pressures when adding good-fit books to our collection. It is just not professionally responsible *to act on those pressures*. The pressures we should act on? Honoring our students' right to representation, affirmation, and hearing accurate historical narratives. Rely on review sources written by librarians and educators, and your own professional collection development training. Craft a clear collection development policy that includes the steps necessary for families requesting the reconsideration of materials. ALA's Office of Intellectual Freedom has resources to help. *Chapter 2: Building a Restorative Space* contains more thoughts on fighting for our students and equity-based values in different school contexts.

Healing Reading Trauma

Julia Torres—phenomenal English educator and librarian—and I have collaborated on ideas and strategies to heal what we've called *reading trauma*. We do not use the word trauma lightly. If trauma can be described as a deeply distressing or disturbing experience, we identified reading trauma as the harm done to students by common literacy practices. Before we can build healing spaces and programs, we need to understand what traumatic reading practices our students may have encountered or may still be encountering in our school spaces, including high-stakes testing, a "classics" fixation, missing or toxic representation, leveling, and shame.

With high-stakes testing, students' literacy growth is filtered through one lens—a numerical score—which is both damaging and not reflective of the breadth and power of literacy. Furthermore, the reliance on test prep and reading only passages downplays the importance of reading stamina and the relationships students develop with novels. A fixation on the "classics" teaches our students that those are the stories that are valued and deemed important enough for discussion, which is erasing our students' identities and modern lived realities. A lack of meaningful representation and also harmful, toxic representation doesn't allow for Dr. Sims Bishop's mirrors to activate for student readers. Trauma-centered narratives can be, well, literally *traumatizing*, especially when they are the only representation made available. Leveling and limiting students' choices can be a real barrier to literacy engagement. So many of our students have been and are being shamed for what they enjoy reading most—most notably graphic novels and manga. We need to educate our stakeholders on the value of comics and manga in addition to overwhelmingly supporting those formats ourselves—with our time, energy, and budgets.

Any student can suffer from reading stress and trauma, but, in our experience, specific communities of students receive the brunt of toxic, traumatic reading practices and spaces: BISOC—Black, Indigenous Students of Color, English Language Learners, disabled students, and LGBTQ+ students. Where identities intersect[6], the harm can be increased exponentially.

Again, Julia and I do not use the word *trauma* lightly, and we also want to acknowledge that the healing we advocate for is through the lens and role of a school librarian. We are not counselors. We've also found that one of the most important collaborative relationships we have in our schools is *with* our counselors. To build healing school spaces, this partnership is essential. Towards this end, we can collaborate on books supporting the mental and SEL health of our students. We can think of our power as librarians in both *macro* and *micro* ways. On the *macro* level, we can collaborate with school counselors on programming and displays promoting books centering mental health realities. On a *micro* level, we can share specific titles with our counselors for them to read and recommend to students they are supporting. Literature is an excellent access point for talking about any topic, including mental health realities. It can be a lower-stakes, more accessible conversation to have about a book character, as opposed to ourselves. Again, this can happen in *macro* ways during classes and clubs, but in *micro* ways when supporting a student one-on-one.

Another way that counselors and school librarians are natural collaborators is that we can both be safe people in our schools. I actually don't claim that my library is a safe place, as I cannot guarantee safety in every moment for every student, especially when I'm in a classroom and not even *in* the library. I can, however, guarantee that I am a safe *person*. For those of us teaching older students who have more autonomy in movement throughout the day, being a safe stopping point for students who are waiting to connect with another staff member—a school counselor, social worker, or psychologist—is powerful. In Chapter 2, the idea of the library being a soft place for students to land was centered. Creating these sorts of spaces in our schools can lessen the load on our school counselors and is a beautiful way to asynchronously partner.

How do we center healing reading practices in our schools to build restorative libraries? We must reframe how we understand student behaviors around reading. For students who have (or do) associate reading with emotional discomfort, insecurity, humiliation, or consistent stress, this can result in readers who appear bored, apathetic, or angry. When we build reading experiences that are not happening under a time constraint, not used as a measure of comparison, and not happening simply to be prepared for an assessment, we start opening up our students—all of our students—to what literacy can be.

We cannot force our students into becoming readers. Instead, we can remove the barriers preventing that natural relationship between story and student from naturally developing. As human beings, we are drawn to stories! Connecting all of our students to beautiful stories that they can connect with is possible. It's probable. And, it's necessary! How do we interrupt traumatic reading practices and remove barriers to reading? When we establish our role as librarians as caretakers of our students and their literacy—and not the books on our shelves—we are establishing a more healing library. Dr. Kim Parker asked: "Do we care about the book or do we care about the reader?"[7] In each moment, each context, this is a key question to live by. Every time—in terms of policy, interactions, physical layout, advocacy—we have to choose the reader, the student.

Additionally, we can establish healing reading practices through building inclusive libraries. Remember that a foundational healing reading practice *is* our reflective collection. Jani L. Barker found that providing reflective literature to BISOC can actually provide healing from the damage of living in a racist society.[8]

It goes without saying that shame should have no part in our libraries. No shame around the types of reading enjoyed—from manga to *Diary of a Wimpy Kid* to romantasy—or the desire to re-read books and series. Celebrate what your students are reading! *Reading is reading is reading*. From fan-fiction to audiobooks to web comics, establish your support for all modes of reading. On my "What I'm Reading Sign" I hang in the library, I permanently have the *Archive of Our Own* fanfiction site logo featured as well as whatever webcomic I'm currently subscribing to right next to the library novels and manga I'm reading. This small micro-affirmation of what I consider reading (everything!) gets frequently and positively commented on by students. Furthermore, work to widen that circle of acceptance and affirmation of all sorts of texts to include classroom teachers, administration, and families.

When we create more opportunities through our library programs which give students time for choice-based reading, we are offering healing reading practices. Whether it is through working with classroom teachers to develop Sustained Silent Reading, DEAR time, book clubs, or projects which center text choices, we are supporting our students' literacy development in ways that have lasting effects.

Last year, I piloted a reading elective in our school that was similar to a silent book club, and I named it *Reclaiming Reading*. (Thank you to librarian Angie Manfredi for that naming idea!) In our elective, we simply read. Whatever we wanted. For the entire 70-minute period. For some students who weren't used to reading in such a sustained way, I scaffolded with quick activities, community builders, and conversations until they built the stamina to read on their own. When that first cohort of students reflected on their reading, they were highlighting the power of this sort of reading freedom.

- *"I learned that I love reading if I'm not forced to."*
- *"I enjoy reading a lot more than i thought."*
- *"The class period at the beginning felt long, but when we got farther into the trimester, the periods felt shorter."*
- *[When asked how they felt when leaving class], "Really good!!! I feel like i've been off my phone a lot since i found books i love reading."*

- *"I thought that reading was boring before the class and now after i gave it a chance, i get lost in books when i read them."*

I shared data from that first elective—including student quotes with permission—with both administration and families. I've since offered this elective again, and it will be a mainstay of my library program each year. Most of the students who take this class do not enroll because they already love reading. Instead, they disclose that this elective is appealing because the library feels welcoming since my arrival. They are simply looking for calm in their stressful days. For me, this highlights the power of making our spaces restorative. Increased reading has naturally been one of the wonderful outcomes we can experience in our schools when we build restorative spaces.

Healing reading practices require joyful consistency. First *joy*. Joy is an element that can be missing from schools, especially as students rise in grade level. As librarians, we can infuse our libraries with joy, from a simple program like sticker Fridays to a space with fidgets and blankets to being an adult for students who is always, always happy to see them. Does a manufactured joy-inducement like stickers work if the library is not a joyful place to begin with? No, of course not. Build joy through your collection and through *you*. From there, the "little" initiatives will mean even more. Then, *consistency*. None of these library practices are healing if we only do them sometimes. It's every student. Every day.

Funding

I'd be remiss if I talk about building restorative collections without mentioning the need for funding. Sustaining a student-centered collection is expensive. I certainly don't have all the answers, but I can share what has worked for me in transforming two distinct collections at two widely varying schools. Should school librarians need to hustle for books that our students want and need? No, of course not. The reality is that with library budgets being slashed and book prices increasing, turning a bargain shopping mentality to buying books will ultimately support the collection goals for your library.

When I started at my first school and literally gutted the stagnant collection of most of its books, I needed to fill the shelves with books my students would want to read. I had a $500 library budget, which is laughable. Even so, I didn't want to touch that money until I had engaged with students and teachers. So how could I still have new, fresh books to welcome students on the first day? This balance is a conundrum that many new librarians face. I wrote a myriad of grants that first summer, including several DonorsChoose grants (donorschoose.org). In addition, I scoured library sales and thrift stores for books in great condition that were engaging and current. It allowed me to start the year with books I was proud to advertise in the hallways to signal that the library was transforming.

After I got to know my students in those first weeks, I quickly spent that $500! As students started visibly engaging with the library and its books, I shared those personal, powerful stories with the administration. I also shared a collection development plan and a minimum amount of book-purchasing funds ($3K) I'd need to continue to support students and their literacy engagement. That first year, I also wrote a grant application for a Laura Bush Foundation Grant and was awarded $7K. With those funds, I jump-started our graphic novel and manga section, purchased inclusive class texts for ELA and Social Studies classes, filled in series, and replaced our non-fiction sections with new books directly related to students' interests and curricular content.

I continued to use DonorsChoose grants throughout my eight years at Mount Vernon—writing over 35 grants that were 100% funded by strangers. In my experience, there are so many people who want to support school libraries, intellectual freedom, and reflective books. Donating through DonorsChoose is a concrete way for people to help. My budget fluctuated depending on the principal and district support, but it never again fell below 3K. To be clear, 3K is not enough, but it was a baseline I needed to build from. The collection I ultimately built at Mount Vernon was beautiful: powerful, reflective, student-centered, and engaging.

When I turned to high school librarianship at my current independent school, Carolina Friends School, I thought my days of scheming and strategizing for book funds were over. I was wrong. While the collection did not need to be gutted, it did need to be heavily weeded and refreshed. In my first year, I tripled the manga section, genrefied non-fiction to de-Dewey it, removed reference books, and made the fiction titles much more reflective of my students. My population had changed and my student demographics represented an increase in neurodivergence and LGBTQ+ identities. My budget at 10K had seemed large, but that number quickly dwindled when I realized that database and news subscriptions would eat most of it. I repeated what I had done at Mount Vernon to transform the collection. I had a two-prong attack: 1) share stories and advocate with leadership to increase my book budget and 2) shop creatively to get the books I needed.

What are the common threads between both schools and their widely different experiences?

- Advocacy with administration by sharing stories about the transformative power of inclusive literature.
- Widely looking for deals on new and used books through distributor sales, resale sites like Thriftbooks.com[9], thrift and consignment stores, and conference "freebies." If ALA, NCTE, or AASL conferences are near enough for you to drive, consider asking for funding to attend with a cheaper exhibits-only pass to load your car with books from the exhibit hall that you can use to add to your collections or—in the case of ARCs—add to your #TrueBookFAIR stash (see Chapter 10).

There is a certain satisfaction to the hustle of finding great used books. Not only are we stretching our budget dollars, but we're pulling our libraries in a sustainable direction, too.

LEVERAGE YOUR EXPERTISE

- What collection strategies do you already use to build an inclusive collection? Identify a framework from this chapter to cement and/or expand your collection strategies.
- Are you a weeding champion? Consider offering your skills to colleagues who may struggle with this part of the job. If you're on the opposite end of the spectrum, what possible weeding partners can you identify to help?
- What opportunities for independent reading already exist in your school or library? What could you add to offer even more restorative reading time?
- What healing literacy practices are centered in your library? Which could you add or strengthen?

Gardens

People often use the metaphor of gardens to describe how important it is to weed our library shelves. I also like to think of our libraries as gardens in that we are growing readers. There is an old story in which someone asked a gardener why her plants grew so beautifully. The gardener responded: *I don't force them to grow. I remove what stops them.* This encapsulates how I feel about students growing into humans who love to read. I don't force students to read. Instead, I remove all the elements that are stopping them from growing.

Notes

1 Bishop, R. S. (1990). Mirrors, windows, and sliding glass doors. *Perspectives: Choosing and Using Books for the Classroom*, 6(3), ix–xi.

2 Adichie, Chimamanda Ngozi. "The Danger of a Single Story." *Ted: Ideas Worth Spreading*, July 2009, www.ted.com/talks/chimamanda_adichie_the_danger_of_a_single_story.
3 Lo, M. (2015). *Recommended Read: The Third Twin by CJ Omololu.* Malinda Lo Blog, February 24, 2015.
4 Nandini Islam, T. (2016). How Do You Write About "Diversity" When the Word Has Become Hollow? Elle, March 24, 2016.
5 Paris, D. (2018). *International Literacy Association Keynote.* Austin, TX, July, 2018.
6 Crenshaw, Kimberlé. (1989). "Demarginalizing the intersection of race and sex: a Black feminist critique of antidiscrimination doctrine, feminist theory and antiracist politics". *University of Chicago Legal Forum.* University of Chicago Law School, 1989: 139–168.
7 Parker, K. (2019). *Putting Diverse Books into Practice.* Harvard Graduate School of Education Edcast, September 25, 2019.
8 Barker, J. (2010). Racial identification and audience in *Roll of Thunder, Hear My Cry* and *The Watsons Go to Birmingham—1963. Children's Literature in Education*, 41, 118–145.
9 At ThriftBooks, you can even "sell" your weeded books through their BuyBack program for credit to purchase new and used books.

4

Restorative Policies and Procedures

No doesn't appear in our library space; it does not have a starring role in our policies and procedures. The goal is not permissiveness, but community. After all, how we frame the administrative workings of our libraries is just as important as our collections and our spaces in building a healing library program. We can remove barriers to access and literacy by examining our circulation policies, replacing rules with community norms, and relying on student-centered procedures.

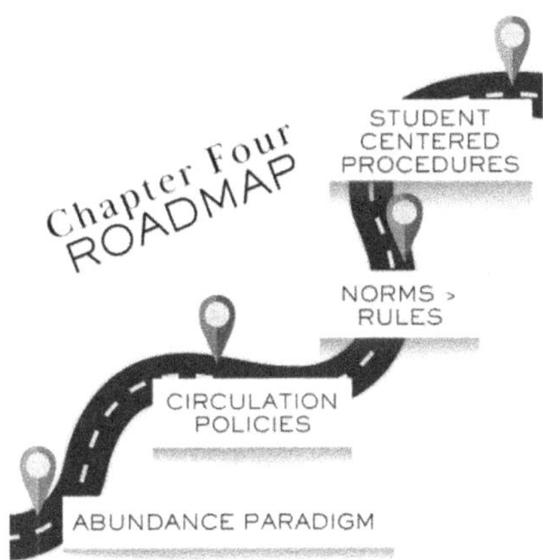

DOI: 10.4324/9781003564775-5

When we view our library policies through the lens of an abundance paradigm versus a scarcity mentality, it can help us reframe how we prioritize our library resources. In the words of Tala Manassah, a scarcity mentality is a "paradigm of the world that says that there are limited resources and we are in a zero-sum game to compete for them. This includes material things, but also things like recognition, credit, and power. An abundance paradigm, on the other hand, proposes the opposite: there is enough to go around and that everyone benefits when justice, resources, visibility, and love are shared."[1] Viewing our library policies through an abundance paradigm is an extremely helpful framework in building an equity-based library. Can schools make up for the inequities that occur outside of school? No, but we can ensure that we are not adding to inequities or exacerbating them further.

Circulation Policies

Traditional circulation policies are driven by a scarcity mentality where the number of books students are able to check out at a time are limited, overdue fines are levied, and students are punished for lost books. Using an abundance paradigm for how we consider our circulation policies—at first glance—might seem impossible given the funding difficulties that we face as school librarians. I am not suggesting that we have a flippant relationship with the stewardship of the books in our libraries. Instead, I want us to remember that it's much better to lose a book than a reader.

Strict check-out limits—for example, allowing students to check out only one book at a time—do not make sense for many students. If a student is checking out books in a manga series to read over the weekend, one book is not going to cut it! This example conversation illustrates my check-out policies and can work for both middle and high school students.

- *We all have different success levels with keeping track of our things. I want you to be able to check out as many books as you know you can keep up with. If for you, that's one, great! Check out just one book at a time. If you like to read from several different formats at a time, maybe you know you can keep track of a guide about birds, a fantasy title, and your favorite graphic novel to re-read, then check out three. For me, I know I'll lose books if I take too many out at a time, so I usually limit myself to two.*

- I then give them think time about how many books they think they can keep up with, then continue.
- *If I have another student who is really waiting for a book you have checked out and you've had it checked out for a long time, I might come ask you about it. If you find yourself not being able to keep up with the amount of books you've checked out, we'll brainstorm a way to move forward. You won't be in trouble. We'll come up with solutions together.*

Restorative elementary circulation procedures shared by NC colleague Angie Headley offer a similar approach. To teach our youngest library users, Angie lays a foundation on how to use a library and begins with a one-book checkout for Kindergarteners. This provides a positive, first experience with some helpful limits and avoids punitive conversations with students or families. She then gradually releases the limits and by the end of the year, kindergarteners and also first and second graders are checking out up to three books at a time. Angie's approach for third through 5th grade mirrors mine.

A restorative stance on overdue fines is simple—*do not do it*. Even public libraries are dialing back on charging fines and late fees. Overwhelmingly, libraries have found that removing fines did not cause books to be returned any later or for more books to be lost.[2] Instead, they have found that books are being returned more efficiently after they removed the threat of fines. School libraries that charge fines do not really affect all students who have overdue books. They are only truly punishing students and families who are financially struggling. To what end are we doing this? What may have the intention of "teaching responsibility" instead has the impact of causing anxiety and humiliation.

Having the possibility—or threat—of fines hanging over the heads of students will prevent some of them from checking out books at all. In this way, fines are a concrete barrier to access. They also can lead some students to associate library books with shame or embarrassment—particularly our most economically vulnerable students who may need our library resources the most. As Chad Donohue says in "Give the Kid a Pencil," students "learn best in a psychologically safe, mistake-friendly environment."[3] Financially charging students for the mistake of an overdue book doesn't build a safe-feeling or restorative library.

When students lose or damage a book, I do not assess a charge for that, either. Instead, it's the start of a conversation. If a student comes to me with a damaged book, I always start by saying,"Thank you. Thank you for trusting me with this mishap." The student will usually want to tell a story which will give time and space to brainstorm on how this kind of damage can be prevented in the future.

If a student tells me a book is lost, I ask them to give one more look at home. We may brainstorm all the places they can look–turning it into a quest instead of a shameful sort of crime. (Unless I know something about their home situation, for example, if I know their family is unhoused. In that situation–I just say *thank you for letting me know—I'll remove it from your circulation account* and then we talk about something unrelated and positive.)

If a student sees a book under their name when they are checking out and gives a knee-jerk reaction of—*I already brought that book in!*—I don't disagree. I'll say something like, "*Oh good! I'll look for it here on my end and you do another sweep of your space on your end. This way, we'll cover all our bases.*"Often, the students will reply with something like: "*Oh, you know what? I think it might be under my bed.*"I've found that approaching any conversation about missing books with curiosity, not judgment, is helpful.

At my first school, our student population was so small, I didn't need to send out automated emails—I could just remind students through conversations. At my current school, I rewrote the automatic emails for overdue books to be less pejorative and more curious. The subject line changed from *Library Books Due* to *Are You Still Reading Your Library Book* ☺? I removed warnings about charges for lost books and replaced it with language that expressed gratitude for checking out a library book and signaled a desire to have the book returned for other readers. If students or families reach out and *want* to replace a lost book, I share a wish-list link so they can purchase what they think is appropriate. I never ask students or families to give the library money to replace a book.

Do I have lost books that need to be replaced out of library budget funds? Yes, yes I do. However, my percentage of lost books has historically been no higher than schools with stricter policies. What led me to be so firm on not asking for families to replace lost books?

In my first year as a middle school librarian, I encountered so many students who were scared to check out a book because they claimed,"I have a book on my record." First, I moved to change the language around this as the use of the word "record" was troubling and sounded like a criminal charge. When I would look into their account, I would see that often it was a lost book from early elementary school that carried a high charge. Many students hadn't checked out a book since then—seven or eight *years*—because either they were not allowed to by a former school policy, their families forbade it, or the student themselves did not want anything else on their "record." The first thing I'd tell my students—in their very first circulation visit of the year—is that they can always check out a book from our library. Next, that we'd solve the problem on their *account* together. I would communicate with the school associated with the lost book and beg/cajole the librarian to remove the book from the student's account. I was determined that every student would have an account devoid of lost books or fines before they left me. Any charge on a student's account could prevent them from participating in future school activities like prom or even graduation!

Also, in my first year—in a very large district—a message thread appeared on our librarian listserver that expressed frustration with the number of books never returned by unhoused students in McKinney-Vento programming. The librarian was bemoaning the fact that as students moved between housing locales, the books would be "lost." I saw this message thread over ten years ago, but I can still remember my fury in crafting a response that reminded all of us that we were talking about youth that did not have a stable home—or any home. Who cares about a book that doesn't come back to us? Not only could it have been impossible for a student to manage holding on to the book, but a student could have voluntarily chosen to bring it to their new locale. If the latter was true, what a gift for us as librarians! That something we provided carried a feeling of consistency or care that was deep enough to travel with a student. In this case, I suggested, the book isn't lost. It has simply *found a new home*. The way forward was and is clear: remove the book from the student's account and replace it in your collection if necessary. If we don't have enough money in our schools to provide books to students without homes, then what are we even doing?

Circulation policies are often the most visible aspect of our library to families and can have a lasting impact on a family's relationship with libraries in general. It's an honor for us to create positive, restorative experiences not only for our students, but for their families as well. We do not want the only communication a family ever receives from the library to be an overdue notice. On the contrary, we can provide newsletters, positive calls home, and information on restorative programming such as #TrueBookFAIRs (see Chapter 10).

Community Norms

Not only does our library not feature the word no, it also does not post rules—such as *no eating, no swearing, no yelling*. In my experience, rules are just something to cause stress for the rule-followers and an interesting challenge for the rule-pushers with a threat of punishment for all. Instead of rules, I rely on community norms. The message here is: *this is how we do things for the good of us all*.

Even though it is just a slight language switch, I've discovered that it's had a real impact. To demonstrate how students absorb this language and concept, I'd love to tell you a quick story about a student at Mount Vernon that I'd had for all three years—which was rare in our alternative school. Often, students would transition back to their base school after a year with us. Pedro was a student who knew me—and our library—well. He was there before school started, doing puzzles with me, he always ate lunch in the library, and had signed up for clubs and STEAM activities I had hosted. Pedro was a kid who knew how our library worked. Late in his 8th-grade year, we were in the library during lunch, and a student threw food from his lunch across the space, attempting to hit the trash can. Several students admonished him—*dude, you can't do that in here*—and I told him casually to come clean up the mess and reminded him (momentarily forgetting about my chosen rule nomenclature) by saying—*c'mon (insert name), that's like a hard library rule to not throw food*. Pedro *gasped*, yelling out: *Wait! You have rules here?* Pedro knew throwing food was not okay, but he didn't consider it a *rule*; rather, it was just how we did things in the library, together.

I handle Community Norms in a different way to how I handle Community Agreements. At the beginning of each year in my Fandoms and Interests Survey (see *Chapter 7: Marketing = Seeing*), I solicit student input on norms for the library. I may then add norms to reflect what physically works best for the space and for our school community. For example, even if one year a student doesn't suggest including a community norm about not using hateful language or slurs, I will still include that! Norms are listed on my Google Classroom site, our internal library website, and I vocalize them to students during orientation each year. Norms may change from year to year, but always include similar language to:

- Your reading lives are important. This library will curate materials to reflect you and your interests.
- To build a community in our library, we will treat each other gently.
  - We'll use language that shows consideration for who we each are and our hobbies and activities.
  - We'll use chosen pronouns and names.
  - Slurs and hateful language are never welcome.

- We'll each clean up after ourselves, showing care for the time and dignity of the people who clean our school buildings.

For Community Agreements around a club, class, or specific issue (like eating), I'll create those intentionally in-person with students and we'll either verbally agree, thumbs-up or sign to them (myself included). In "Using Community Agreements to Start the Year Strong,"[4] Cait O'Connor outlines a restorative way to develop community agreements together and hers is guidance I've used in the past several years for clubs and classes. I especially appreciate how she treats the word "respect" with students. "Respect is a word that can be amorphous when we use it or demand it from others, especially in the educational realm, where it often comes with a power differential: It's expected by those with more power and given by those with less power." We can have students unpack the word respect with specific examples that are then explicitly stated in our agreements.

Student-Centered Procedures

To prioritize students in libraries, I've had to get used to saying *no* to adults. It's ironic because I'm very good at saying *yes* to students. Our school libraries are often pleasing spaces and I've found that they can be conscripted for adult purposes at increasingly alarming levels as the year progresses. In my first school, there were all-day (!) district meetings that the librarian before me didn't know she could say no to. I said no. I shared all the reasons why closing a hub of literacy for students at an academic-recovery school was ill-advised and irresponsible. The meetings stopped after that first year. At my current school, there are requests for adult meetings or HR interviews in the library's conference room that is a prime hang-out spot for students during lunch time. Again, I had to say no to protect my students' ability to have their own space for clubs and/or casual lunches.

Again, I shared reasons why this time and space is sacred to students. In every case, I refuse to believe that there are no other spaces for these kinds of meetings to happen. I suspect that it is librarians' sense of organization and space curation that dooms us to these requests (or even demands). I'm not suggesting that we not support our colleagues. I am suggesting that supporting our students should always come *first*.

Another way we can practice student-centered librarianship is by noticing what students need and listening to their requests, changing library procedures when necessary. When I arrived at my current school, I discovered that eating was not allowed in the library. This baffled me because our school does not have a cafeteria or area for students to eat. In my first few weeks, I noticed that students would eat outside on a walkway and then come into the library for lunch. Adults told me it absolutely had to be this way because,"Students will make a mess" and "There will be 'roaches." These are *high school* students they were talking about. After including a question about changing library procedures in my initial survey, I reached out to all of the students who requested a change in where students can eat. We then created a set of agreements together for eating in the library. I advertised the upcoming change in our announcements and requested that all students had to do in order to eat in the library moving forward was to read and sign the community agreements to care for the space and each other. Students were thrilled. Almost two years later, and we're still eating in the library. I have wipes and paper towels readily available. I occasionally need to gently remind students to clean, but in general, it has been a complete non-issue. I have yet to see a roach.

These are two concrete examples of student-centered librarianship, but truly, this way of being in the library happens in a multitude of small ways all the time. We can look at every library reality from the lens of students: does this benefit and care for them, their time, their energy, their physical selves? To build a restorative library, this sort of constant reflection from us is both a helpful and necessary activity.

LEVERAGE YOUR EXPERTISE

- In what ways does your library already live out an abundance paradigm? Are there any aspects of your library program that represent a scarcity mentality?
- When you assess your circulation policies, how are your most vulnerable students and families affected?
- What library norms are made visible in your space—either print or in digital spaces like learning management systems or websites?
- Count the number of times the word NO appears in your library space. Are there opportunities to flip the framing on how norms are established?
- In what ways do your students have a voice in library procedures? In what additional ways could their voices be elevated and their desires for the space be honored?

To restore students' relationships with reading and libraries, we can use an abundance paradigm as we facilitate our library programs. The more times we can communicate *yes* instead of *no* with students and families through our policies and procedures, the more of an inclusive, restorative community we can build.

Notes

1 Manassah, T. (2019). A New Vision of School. *Morningside Center for Teaching Social Responsibility*, May 5, 2019.
2 Unrein, S. (2020). "Overdue Fines: Advantages, Disadvantages, and How Eliminating Them Can Benefit Public Libraries." *iSchool Public Libraries Initiative*. School of Information Studies at Syracuse University. April, 2020.
3 Donohue, C. (2016). "Give the Kid a Pencil." *Learning for Justice*. Southern Poverty Law Center, August 4, 2016.
4 O'Connor, C. (2021). "Using Community Agreements to Start the Year Strong." *Edutopia*, August 24, 2021.

5

Restorative Instruction + Collaboration

With Beth Campbell

School librarians teach; and we teach, a lot. Depending on the grade levels of our students and whether our schedule is fixed, flexible, or hybrid, we may find ourselves teaching library lessons and instruction, partnering with a content or grade-level teacher on a literacy or research unit, and/or teaching or co-teaching our own specialized electives. To ensure that we are teaching well, it is vital to understand and use culturally relevant and sustaining teaching methods in both our own instruction and when we collaboratively co-teach.

DOI: 10.4324/9781003564775-6

Culturally Relevant and Sustaining Strategies

As Django Paris and H. Samy Aim explain, culturally sustaining pedagogy "positions dynamic cultural dexterity as a necessary good, and sees the outcome of learning as additive, rather than subtractive, as remaining whole rather than framed as broken, as critically enriching strengths rather than replacing deficits."[1] How can our work as librarians honor and enrich the "dynamic cultural dexterity" of our students? Culturally sustaining practices in our school libraries can include:

- Being format-open: acknowledging the power of graphic novels, comic books, manga, audiobooks, and fan-fiction in our students' reading lives.
- Building a BIPOC-sustaining, Queer-affirming, Disability-positive, Mental Health-sensitive collection, foregrounding literature that is authored by members of the communities centered in the novels.
- Welcoming multiple languages.
- Engaging learners in setting norms for the library space.
- Centering Black Joy (and Latinx Joy, AAPI Joy, Native Joy, Queer Joy, Disability Joy) and not limiting representation to struggle/trauma.
- Maintaining a collection that reflects our student population and the wide diversity of our country/world.
- Continually and authentically gathering feedback from students on what they want to read.
- Having a space where every student can see themselves visually on library walls and shelves (permanently) and in displays (ever-changing).

With colleague and powerful librarian Chris Tuttell, I embarked on a multi-year study of Zaretta Hammond's *Culturally Responsive Teaching and the Brain* led by our district's Equity Office. As the only librarians in our cohort, we were determined to tailor our learning from the text into specific implications for school librarian practice. As we read Hammond's work, we found that it both cemented and expanded our understanding of how students learn. Culturally responsive teaching is not an adaptive fix or engagement strategy. It is a foundational approach to teaching that supports rigorous cognitive development in our students. "The point is that one's culture, especially one's deep cultural roots, is part of how the brain makes sense of the world and helps us function in our environment."[2]

Culturally responsive teaching and the neuroscience behind learning can thrive through our school library instruction and classroom collaborations with a library-specific foundational toolbox of ideas and practices. This "toolbox" is just that—a collection of ideas and practices that we have used in our libraries and classrooms. There is no list that "does" culturally responsive teaching. It should be a foundation of all of our pedagogical and library practices. Culturally responsive teaching cannot be sprinkled on top of our library practice—it must *be* our practice.

Additionally, culturally responsive librarians must dedicate time—consistently and continually—doing the necessary internal work to combat internal bias and grow our own equity capacity. Project READY—a free, online, self-paced anti-racist curriculum for librarians—is a powerful tool no matter where you are on your own equity journey (ready.web.unc.edu).

An instructional toolbox for culturally relevant library instruction can include:

- Seeking out nontraditional texts to use during instruction, including comics, manga, videos, spoken word, student writing, lyrics, and contemporary poetry.
- Having an asset-driven perspective—as opposed to a deficit model way of thinking—for parents, families, and communities, and recognizing their funds of knowledge.
- Recognizing a range of literacy gifts, from rhyming to drawing to creative writing to improv to rapping to debate.
- Providing choice—as often as possible—for texts, activities, projects, and other summative assessments.
- Stressing collaborative activities, as opposed to competition.

- Welcoming physical movement during instruction—across grade levels!
- Working to help teachers select alternate texts to the "traditional literary canon" to foreground literature that reflects our students, their lived experiences, and/or their interests (while recognizing that racial groups are not monoliths). #DisruptTexts—and the scholarship of Tricia Ebarvia, Lorena Germán, Dr. Kimberly N. Parker, and Julia Torres—is essential reading for this work (https://disrupttexts.org).

Collaborations

Collaborating with classroom and grade-level teachers is not only an official shared foundation from our National School Library Standards (standards.aasl.org), but it is also a vital way we can build restorative library programs. I've been lucky enough to collaborate with wonderful educators, and I invited my first true collaborator to unpack what makes classroom/library collaborations so meaningful.

When I started at Mount Vernon, Beth Campbell was the 7th-grade science teacher. Beth has over 25 years of educational experience and is a certified teacher in seven different content areas, spanning elementary, middle, and high school levels. In our time sharing a school, we collaborated on multiple lessons, units, field trips, electives, and even across subject areas. She is a brilliant teacher. We connected several times to write this section of the chapter together. After all, how could I write a chapter about meaningful and restorative collaboration *by myself*? What felt most authentic to the way collaboration actually works was for us to bounce ideas and memories of our experience back and forth to capture why collaboration can be a restorative practice in schools.

BETH: The first day back to school in January after winter break is my teacher kryptonite. When that alarm goes off, my first thought is always how very *dark* it is outside, and how I'm not entirely sure I remember what the sun looks like.

JULIA: (laughing) It is a very tough day.

BETH: I had this project I'd done as my students and I returned from break that I knew had promise and you had just started as our librarian and had offered to collaborate on anything. I thought your expertise could help strengthen Scientific Discoveries.

JULIA: Ah, the Greenland Shark project!

BETH: Nope, we're not doing this. It was the *Scientific Discoveries Project*. Don't start with the shark.

JULIA: (laughing) You can't deny the power of the Greenland Shark! You came to me in December about the project, right? So we had it planned out before break.

BETH: Honestly, when I did it by myself before you came to Mount Vernon, it was fluff. It was this nice, week-long buffer where each student selected a discovery or breakthrough in the field of science that had made news in the previous year. They researched, pulled key details and images together, and shared their new expertise. It was interesting, timely, and engaging…but it was also a cop-out. This project was born from exhaustion and it showed. In theory, it had potential, but it wasn't planned or delivered terribly well.

JULIA: It was such a cool idea! I was excited to jump on board.

BETH: So, with you there, I could still capitalize on the benefits of it being high interest, of it being timely and relevant. You raised the bar so much. You provided more structure and more responsible research. Then, their projects shared information about what they had learned in a careful and considered way. It took it from being me, mailing it in a little bit to me feeling like I was really building community and welcoming those students back with an engaging, dare I say, *rigorous* project.

JULIA: Rigorous has been weaponized so much with us as educators on the ground that it's hard not to eye-roll sometimes, but yes, we created a truly rigorous project with high-level vocabulary, a final project that stretched them, and research they had to actively engage with—all with scaffolding.

BETH: And then we made that huge hallway display, right, that our admin kept showing off? With the students' research?

JULIA: Yes, I loved that project! But, Beth, that wasn't the first thing we collaborated on. It's funny because you remember that project as my work being so special ,and I'm like—what, I just helped with research and projects? No big deal. What was meaningful to *me* was that you came and asked me about making a science-fiction display for your classroom with main characters who looked like our students. School librarians are inundated with requests about chromebooks and printers in the beginning of the year, so to have a science teacher come and ask me about books? About reflective books? You were speaking my library love language and I knew I would have a partner for equity work.

BETH: Oh wow—I know just what you are talking about, but I didn't think of that as collaboration before—I thought of it as advice from an expert. Isn't it funny how collaboration comes in so many varied forms?

JULIA: Yes, and it's all worthwhile. It's all additive to both of our…school spheres.

BETH: And since you brought up the Greenland Shark, let's talk about that for a sec. To me, one of the best things about collaborating with another educator is that we double the chances that our students will feel seen and heard. Often, classrooms are set up in a way that implies that the teacher's perspective and opinions are more valid, which can be harmful to students' sense of self. Adding a second adult to the room creates situations where the teacher's views can be safely and respectfully challenged, or called out, for the bias that is often present. This fosters a restorative environment where students can see diversity of thought in a way that is likely to validate their own ideas.

JULIA: Co-teaching feels more restorative for everyone involved.

BETH: Definitely. So back to the shark. One of the scientific breakthroughs students could choose to research was the recent discovery that a species of shark was living to be over four hundred years old. The shark discovery seemed trivial to me among the other topics that caught my attention—most of which were ground-breaking accomplishments of human intellect and effort. The shark just…lived for a while. But then I sat back and watched as you and Brian, one of our students, both got wide-eyed, leaning into each other, taking turns coming up with world events spanning multiple human lifetimes while one ancient Greenland Shark swam through ocean depths. It was beautiful. That opportunity—the excitement and validation and connection that student felt wouldn't have happened if you hadn't been in the room.

JULIA: You introduced the Greenland Shark scientific news last. And, I thought, of course! She's clearly saving the best project idea for last. And, you said to me as an aside, ugh, that shark. I just wanted one more idea so I threw it in. (Laughing.) I love co-teaching. There is that cliché that sorrows shared are halved and joys are doubled? I think that is usually true when educators get to co-teach.

BETH: Often, we as classroom teachers co-plan a lesson with another teacher or a team or our PLC, but when you step over the threshold into your classroom, you're alone. But, with you, building those lessons together and then delivering them together, I just loved it. It was powerful having someone with me to bear witness to how our shared vision transitioned into meaningful learning in real time.

JULIA: And, then to get to reflect on the lessons together to unpack how they went? What we noticed about what worked and didn't? Working with you improved my own teaching so much.

BETH: And, our professional partnership modeled to students how to work together, too, don't you think?

JULIA: Yes! As educators, we expect our students to collaborate, but how often do we model it in front of them?

BETH: And logistically, it is a gift to have another professional to support students when they are working independently.

JULIA: Students would want Ms. Campbell or want Ms. Stivers depending on their question, but do you remember what Juan said? *"I want whoever will pay attention to me."*He was new to us at Mount Vernon, had only been with us maybe a month? That was ten years ago and I still think about it. *Whoever will pay attention to me.* When we collaborate, we can literally pay attention to more students in the classroom at any given moment.

BETH: And, somehow it always ends up being the students who need it most.

JULIA: And then we did our big Paideia/GMO project. I mean the Greenland Shark was just a warm-up.

BETH: After the success of *Scientific Discoveries*, I was so excited to look ahead in the curriculum and map out where else we could collaborate. My next unit was about genetics, and there was a section about selective breeding and genetically modified organisms. At the time, GMOs were a frequent news topic, with debate about the science, the safety, and even morality of modifying living things. We taught students who had a history of academic challenges, and I relished the idea that they might have a chance to be the smartest person in the room if or when the topic came up outside of school.

JULIA: Yes, I remember when you came to me, you said you wanted them to have a chance to form a research-based opinion, and be able to articulate and defend it.

BETH: Exactly. Middle schoolers are all about opinions and arguments, so developmentally, it is a great time for them to learn to research the facts behind controversial topics, and weave them into a logic-based claim.

JULIA: Helping the students understand both the science and public opinion and then forming their own ideas, backed by research—this was such a perfect project for collaboration.

BETH: It truly was. I decided to have a Paideia Seminar so we had a venue for our arguments and space for disagreement, but with high expectations for respectful discourse and a willingness to hear differing viewpoints.

JULIA: I was excited about this because it honored the verbal gifts of a lot of our students in a way an assessment like a test wouldn't have.

BETH: I was super excited about the big picture, and you helped me break the project down into actionable steps, and develop learning activities to build both skills and knowledge.

JULIA: And then you moved to FACS [Family and Consumer Science].

BETH: And, then I moved to FACS. And I was totally thrown for a loop, teaching in an entirely new content area. It turns out, collaboration with you was exactly what I needed again! Our collaborations were different because we were creating entirely new units together, instead of you transforming a unit I'd already taught.

JULIA: Getting to create the unit on family was my favorite.

BETH: We got to affirm and celebrate all different types of families.

JULIA: Do you remember the images of different families I included? The last slide had Naruto's family and some of the students fake fainted.

BETH: (laughing) In happiness.

JULIA: Yes. Excitement. Look, if I can add anime into a lesson, *I'm going to*. But, seriously, leveraging what I know about students' interests into a lesson to make it more relatable? I love that. And, I think librarians can really shine at that.

BETH: And it helps us so much! And, that was the unit where I decided to openly mock my curriculum in front of my students. I was shocked when I was expected to teach a specific definition of "family," as if it was an academic vocab word like "cell membrane" or "hypotenuse."

JULIA: And to make things worse, there was also a list of "types of families," each with their own label and definition—and I think the whole list had maybe four types, right?

BETH: (exasperated) Yes! And looking at our students, I knew about half of them had lived experiences, people they called family, that didn't fit into those cookie cutter definitions and I was NOT about to invalidate their families by teaching definitions that excluded them. I knew I had an ally in you and your support gave me the courage to approach this topic in a way that pushed back against the assumptions, biases, and limitations of my curriculum.

JULIA: I'm always here to throw-out biased curriculum with anyone. Anytime.

BETH: And, then I had a surprise observation right when we were starting!

JULIA: From an administrator who was very 'by the book' and wanted standards written on the board no matter how student un-friendly the language was.

BETH: I almost rolled things back, but I didn't! Largely because you were there, and I knew you had my back, along with the research to support it! And, then he spoke from the heart about his own family and adoption. It felt transformative.

JULIA: We were always intentional with resources, centering experts and practitioners who looked like our students. I love how you collaborate with community members and experts no matter your subject. And, always, always searching out partners whose identities and backgrounds reflect our students.

BETH: We both do that! As white educators working with majority BIPOC students, collaboration has to include BIPOC community partners.

JULIA: Absolutely. And, not in a way that is asking for unpaid labor or time!

BETH: We have collaborated so much, it's easy to connect and dive into any topic. But, what do you do when you're collaborating with a teacher you don't connect with?

JULIA: As librarians, we're going to collaborate with so many different personalities and perspectives in schools. I've never finished collaborating on a lesson or project and felt regret that I'd done it. It's always valuable. Even when—maybe even especially when—I'm collaborating with a teacher whose equity goals or understanding of anti-bias teaching do not align with mine, it's an opportunity. Yes, an opportunity to model and nudge a teacher in a more anti-racist, accurate historical direction, but also an opportunity to be another adult in the room.

BETH: We both know you've had to co-teach with some um… unenlightened folks.

JULIA: Sometimes collaborations are about advocating for students—by either getting novels and topics in the curriculum that reflect them and their interests or by helping teachers see what they need on an individual basis. Or, honestly, both.

BETH: I've seen you gently help teachers with remembering students' names and pronouns. And model using more inclusive language.

JULIA: As educators, I think we all generally want to improve. Modeling inclusive language whether it's using ungendered terms or using more historically correct terms like enslaver instead of master or owner…I'm super intentional in how I model that to teachers. I've had the most success with using it clearly and in the case of enslaver—explaining to students why I'm using it instead of what's in the text book for example—and then the teacher will just start using the updated language too.

BETH: It's strange though because I think of you as a bold person, but you are very gentle in the way you collaborate.

JULIA: To collaborate well and get into classrooms where we can do the most work with students, takes a lot of humility. I've seen staff who 'push in' to classrooms literally…um push in. Take over. I have the utmost respect for classroom teachers. I always want to honor their classrooms. So, for example, even if I was working with a middle school American History teacher who didn't build his curriculum in a way that lived up to the historical teaching principles of *Learning for Justice* or *Facing History*, to gain entrance to that classroom and the students, I of course still treated the teacher as the content expert in the room. I had respect for what an American History class could be, should be. I just…um nudged him and shared resources to try to move the needle.

BETH: Look, I love teachers. But, not every teacher is a good teacher, and not every teacher is going to make every student feel comfortable. And I see librarians' power in the way you can show up for kids. And I feel like there's something to be said for you joining that student in the experience of being in that teacher's classroom.

JULIA: That's true. And, again, this is not the norm. I work with amazing teachers. Sometimes kids in a classroom are just not feeling seen by certain teachers that might have particular biases that they're not aware of. If I can be a co-teacher in that space and honor that student, it's meaningful.

BETH: Librarians have the potential to be every kid's advisor.

JULIA: (laughing) Yes. We're both firm believers in every student having at least one adult in the school who will be *their* person. Teachers, counselors, learning specialists… are all so good at this. And, librarians can really help fill in the gaps. We can see kids because they share their interests with us and that is such an avenue to connection.

BETH: Not every collaboration is going to look like ours.

JULIA: (laughing) No, I've only achieved this kind of top-of-the-pyramid collaboration from design to planning to co-teaching to reflection with a couple of teachers. But, collaboration is not an all or nothing situation! Every collaboration is valuable. For some teachers, it's sharing resources or making a website. I love doing this because even if I never get into that classroom, I get to push for more culturally relevant materials and then design and share those materials, knowing they are going to be used.

BETH: In terms of literature, historical figures, perspectives?

JULIA: Yes, and sometimes it feels super subtle. Just last week, a teacher asked me to update something another librarian had made on resources about Gaza, called 'Israel-Gaza Events: Resources for Learning.' The first thing I changed was the name of the doc to 'Genocide in Gaza: Resources for Learning.'

BETH: So maybe not so subtle.

JULIA: Maybe not. Then it was reframing the whole doc and the resources chosen. There is immense power in this at our schools. This is why collaboration is a part of a restorative library. How we collaborate can help restore…or it can cause more harm.

BETH: If we were going to wrap up with what makes library collaborations restorative, what would we say?

JULIA: One, it improves instruction.

BETH: Two, it builds community.

JULIA: Okay, yours is better. (laughing) That should be number one. Collaboration done well does build community, between teachers and also between the co-teachers and students.

BETH: And it builds community beyond that classroom. Which strengthens relationships in the entire school. I think because teachers are so relationship-oriented, there can also be exclusionary relationships. We can have our circles—by content or grade level or even location in the school. When we cross those boundaries, those new partnerships can have a real impact on staff.

JULIA: And anything positively impacting staff should have a positive impact on students.

BETH: Yes! Three, it raises accountability. Accountability that we're teaching well, that we're teaching in a way that is culturally competent.

JULIA: When we collaborate, we can see students better, I think. Literally seeing students in different school spaces highlights all of their different kinds of genius. Recognizing and celebrating that genius is restorative.

Low-Hanging Fruit

We recognize that some opportunities to collaborate have a higher likelihood of success than others, and we want to increase the chances that you will build successful restorative collaborations. Here is a list of suggestions that Beth and I curated together and that we believe are the starting points that are more likely to offer opportunities:

- The singletons. If there are teachers who don't have a department or team that teaches the same thing in the same building, they are probably shouldering more of the planning themselves and would be happy for someone to share the work of mapping a lesson, gathering resources, or creating tools.
- The newbies. The teachers who are new to the school or new to teaching may not have a team or a routine of regular collaboration. The offer to partner with a librarian is likely to be very welcome!
- The team leads or department chairs. Often, teachers in leadership positions are the ones who are likely to be

excited about partnerships and collaborations. Plus, you have a better chance of unlocking a collaboration opportunity that spans an entire grade level or subject area.

- Before or after a field trip. If your school has big trips that include an entire grade level or that span multiple days, the teachers are probably planning classroom experiences that prepare students for the trip, or help them process the experience when they return to school. This is a great time for another viewpoint and another set of hands to do the work. An added bonus is that trips are often planned well in advance, so there is time to propose a well-thought-out partnership!
- School-wide celebrations or recognitions. Whether it's the 100th Day of School or a recognition month like Black History Month, you can help make connections between subjects and/or grade levels. To keep recognition months from feeling performative and/or surface-level, librarians can work to provide depth and substance to move beyond food and traditions to expand with historical counterstories, local history, literature, and themes of social justice and activism.
- Projects and big writing assignments. When in-depth learning experiences span multiple days and include a complex product, like an essay, presentation, or display, there are often many components that can easily be divided up and shared with collaborators!
- Opportunities that lean into your own expertise and interests. Every librarian specializes in different aspects or themes of our profession. There are so many elements to library programs: ranging from picture book read-alouds to inquiry-based learning to 3D printing to poetry to coding. What do you feel confident in? For me, it's selecting a great-fit graphic novel or manga that connects to the students and the curriculum and then getting students engaged with the story. This skill/interest formed the basis of so many of my collaborations!

I am incredibly grateful to Beth for the collaborative work we have done with our students and for her input on this chapter. As librarians, we are doing important work, but we won't succeed if that work is trapped between the shelves of our libraries. Collaborating with classroom teachers is a wonderful way to spread our efforts, and in most cases, amplify our efforts at restoration. This can be especially meaningful when we are collaborating with teachers who have different identities, backgrounds, and approaches to our own. This year, I co-taught an elective, *Exploring Anime*, with Davíd Luna, a brilliant linguist and one of our school's Spanish teachers. Unpacking issues of gender, race, sexuality, and language in anime was made more powerful for our students through our varied lived experiences. Not only is Davíd Mexican-American, he's a member of Gen Z, and I felt lucky to learn from and with him over the course of our work together.

I've been lucky to collaborate with Beth, Davíd, and a myriad of other wonderful teachers—Abra, Casey, Mia, Rachel, Sean, Holly. In all of our schools, I am excited about the partnerships we can develop to build connections and community.

LEVERAGE YOUR EXPERTISE

- In what ways do culturally relevant strategies show up in your library instruction? What bullets from the toolbox of ideas could be incorporated into additional programs or lessons?
- What are some of the richest collaborations you have done with educators in your schools?
- What new collaboration activities rose up for you when reading the Low Hanging Fruit section?
- What expertise and interests do you have that you could embed into the curriculum through a collaborative lesson with a classroom teacher?

Notes

1 Paris, D. and Alim, H.S. (2017). *Culturally Sustaining Pedagogies.* New York: Teachers College Press.
2 Hammond, Z. (2015). *Culturally Responsive Teaching and the Brain: Promoting Authentic Engagement and Rigor Among Culturally and linguistically Diverse Students.* Thousand Oaks, CA: Corwin Press.

6

Restorative Practices Embedded in a Library Program

The word *restorative* has a Latin root—*restaurare*—meaning to repair, rebuild, or renew. I'd gladly claim all of those verbs as aspirations for my school library. When we can *repair* students' relationships with reading, *rebuild* their connections with each other, and *renew* their academic energy throughout the school day, we are building restorative school spaces. School librarians can and should have *repair*, *rebuild*, and *renew* as forever goals for our libraries. For those who are guiding our littlest students, you are establishing the positive and powerful foundation of library healing for the rest of us! [Thank you!] In addition to these affirming definitions of *restorative*, the word also has a more specific connotation in relation to educational praxis: restorative practices.

Restorative practices (RP) are broadly defined as "processes that proactively build healthy relationships and a sense of community to prevent and address conflict and wrongdoing" (International Institute for Restorative Practices). Restorative practices are not new. Indigenous communities across the world and Native nations and peoples on this continent were using restorative concepts long before North America was colonized. These (not) "new" educational practices being used today in schools originated with Indigenous and Native communities

DOI: 10.4324/9781003564775-7

hundreds and hundreds of years ago and are still practiced today to restore conflict, repair harm, and build community.

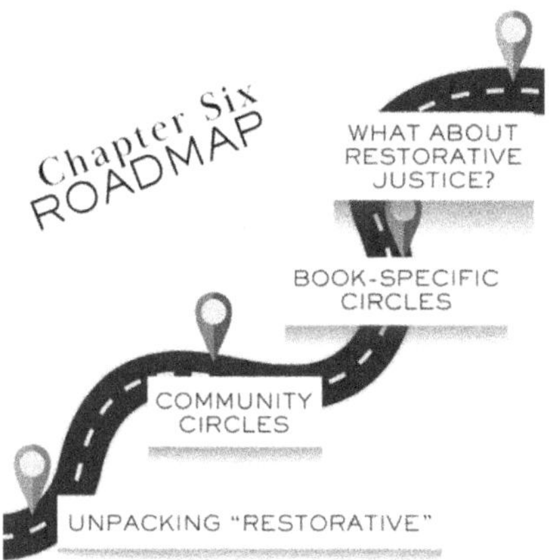

Using restorative practices in our library programs and spaces can offer a myriad of benefits: stronger relationships, more open communication, deeper engagement with learning, a reduction in discipline issues, and increased comfort and well-being for students—and you. Restorative practices must represent a true mindset shift based on unconditional positive regard for students. Adding pieces of RP—such as community circles—into a library program that does not embody anti-racist principles or authentically welcome all students is not going to be successful. Like any equity-minded practice, circles cannot be sprinkled on top of a library practice. Instead, they can be a beautiful part of a library program that is already built on relationships and community.

The Mindset Shift

It's not by chance that this book is called *The Restorative School Library*. Every chapter is intentionally grounded in a way that reflects a restorative way of thinking for our libraries. From making cataloguing decisions that prevent harm to removing lost book fees to transforming a damaging book fair model, every decision in our library can be made with a restorative lens. What does this mean?

- Unconditional positive regard for students.
- Prioritizing relationships over books or rules.
- Building a community with space for all students.
- Goal of eradicating or minimizing harm.
- Seeing every day as an opportunity to affirm and validate students.

In addition to a restorative lens, a specific restorative practice that can be successfully embedded in our library programs is the community circle.

Community Circles

Circles are a cornerstone of restorative practices and my chosen way to structure classroom library visits. Circles can take different forms, including mediation circles to address an issue or problem, healing circles when students are grieving, or community circles for dialogue, storytelling, and engagement. Community circles are the structure I use in my library, and at their core—whether for an advisory period, creative writing exercise, or history discussion—they all strive to build community.

Community circles establish a time and space for me to connect and check in with students. All of our circles follow guidelines that we establish together at the beginning of the year. My specific wording may change from year to year—based on the community norms we establish—but three main concepts are always included:

- No one is required to speak, but every voice is valued. If it's someone's turn to speak and they don't wish to speak or don't have anything to add, they can simply pass to the next person. I've found, though, that often even our quietest students will contribute. The time to process and think is incredibly helpful.
- Learning and lessons can leave the circle, but stories cannot. After trust is built in school communities, students will often share personal stories. These stories cannot be shared by students or me outside of the circle.

- Listen to understand, not respond. Model active listening for students. As your students get used to circles, they will understand that everyone will get a chance to speak. It will eventually be everyone's turn. Students can relax and listen.

It helps to have something in the center of your circle. This gives students something to focus on, especially if they are uncomfortable with eye contact. I often use a selection of books in the circle center.

Community circles can be guided by what is happening in school or outside of it. They can be a way for students to discuss what is important to them and also, of course, provide us with a wonderful opportunity to get to know our students better. Always assess your questions ahead of time, using care to evaluate how they will impact students. Asking students what they did over summer break or a vacation can highlight economic inequities or remind students of trauma. Use questions and prompts that are more trauma-sensitive. Some beginning-of-the-year prompts that I've used are:

- What is one thing you'd like your classmates (or teachers) to know about you?
- What does success look like to you?
- How do you like to be celebrated?
- What is something you're looking forward to this year?
- What is a skill you have that you could teach me how to do?
- What is a subject you wish was going to be taught this year?

Before I started facilitating circles with students, I participated in multiple circles as a participant and attended a multi-day circle keeper training. I've continued to attend training to improve my facilitation skills. I love circles—both participating in them and facilitating them. I've found them to be a fascinating place where all types of students can be comfortable—introverts and extroverts, outgoing talkers and reserved thinkers, both neurotypical and neurodivergent students. Circles can create more equitable sharing time for students. With comments and questions traveling in a circle, quieter students have think time, and your joyful interrupters *know* that their turn is coming. There is safety in knowing that everyone gets a chance to speak and that you're always allowed to pass. Circles can be a restorative part of a school day, but if facilitated irresponsibly or without an equity lens, they can be harmful to our students. Work collaboratively with trained support staff in your building or district—counselors, social workers, psychologists—who have expertise with social-emotional learning and trauma-sensitive practices.

I typically use community circles to jumpstart a lesson. Many ice-breaker questions can be used as prompts to open a circle. In the beginning, I often answer first, but then I will ask for a volunteer to start. Either way, the option to speak or pass then moves in a one-way direction around the circle. The possibilities for questions are limitless. Some of the most popular questions with my students have been:

- What is a hot take you have about food?
- What is a boring fact about yourself?
- What kind of water best represents you today?
- If you could cosplay as a teacher, who would it be?
- If you could snap your fingers and speak a new language, what language would it be?
- If you could hang out with any cartoon character, who would you choose and why?
- What's the best advice you've ever heard?
- If you could pick up a new skill in an instant what would it be?
- What movie can you rewatch over and over again?
- What superpower would you NOT want to have?

For younger students:

- If you could be any animal, what would it be?
- What cartoon character do you wish was real?

- What is something that made you laugh recently?
- What do you think makes a good friend?
- Would you rather have a pet dinosaur or a pet dragon?
- If you had a robot help you with school, but it could only do one task, what would you have it do?
- What are you grateful for today?
- What superpower would you like to have?
- What is something you're really good at?

Community circles build connections when students feel like they are seeing each other and, in turn, being seen and heard, and perhaps even known. Question prompts can continue to go deeper with further questions, or you can move after opening questions into content learning.

In addition to using circles to jump-start a lesson, circles can be used to enhance content learning. Circles can be a low-pressure, but powerful formative assessment tool to check students' understanding of background knowledge or new learning. Any content-related question you would ask at the front of a class can be adapted to ask in a circle. Circles can also be used for content-related discussions.

I've had the most success with using this with history units. For example, 7th-grade social studies educator Abra Rearte and I facilitated circle discussions as a way to discuss the Holocaust and learn key historical concepts in preparation for welcoming survivor Abe Piasek to our school. When we're co-teaching lessons, we can break the class size in half to allow for smaller circles.

Book-Specific Circles

My favorite circles to facilitate are specifically literature-related. I've found that circles add value to circulation visits and that using circulation visits to discuss inclusive literature added value to our circles. We can build circles around any and every circulation visit. Some of my favorite examples are:

Using circles for library orientation. In the center of the circle, have a selection of high-interest books from different sections of the library. Invite each student to select one and spend a minute flipping through their book and noticing one thing about it to share. The thing they notice can be anything: from surface level (a physical attribute) to deeper (making connections with the book's content or author). After enough think time, have everyone hold the book with the front cover facing out and invite comments around the circle. After each person gives their one "noticing" about the book, you can share something about the genre or format it's from. *All of our manga is on the large wall behind me*, or *that's in the horror section, which is on the shelves behind Ash*. It's such a low-pressure way for every student to participate, whether or not they identify as a reader. It's clueing students in that they are all welcome and a part of what we're going to be doing together.

Booktalking a Genre or Theme. Again, you can place a curated selection of books in the center for students to choose from—horror books in October, books about animals for a 4th-grade class related to their current science unit, or WWII historical fiction for a social studies class in the midst of their unit, etc. In this structure, each student could decide whether they wanted to hold the book while you say a few words about the title, or they could choose to lead the book-talk—yes, of course, even if they hadn't read the book! They could read the back, the first few lines, or make comments about the cover or art style. With this approach, booktalking becomes much more interactive and organically invites student voice and input.

History and Awareness Months. With the understanding that learning, celebrations, and awareness for different appreciation months should last all year, you may also be highlighting a selection of books. For example, books written by Native and Indigenous Authors, titles written by Latinx authors, or books centering mental health realities. These circles can again begin with a selection of books in the center for students to select and interactively book-talk with you. You can also invite students to write in a circle. One year, with an 8th-grade class in February, we began by celebrating MG and YA Black authors. Students then wrote down what they wanted to make sure we studied during Black History Month and beyond. I displayed their answers—from Malcolm X to Black Lives Matter to Jason Reynolds to LeBron James to Kehinde Wiley to *Black Panther* to the Black Panthers—in the library and we used the students' list for collaborative English and Social Studies library visits for the rest of the year.

What About Restorative Justice?

Restorative justice is a subset of restorative practices and the way that many people come to learn about RP. Restorative justice focuses on mediation and restitution as opposed to punishment and is a powerful tool for schools to push back against biased and race-based discipline disparities. I'm more focused on RP in this chapter—and my library—as they are built to be proactive and center community and active listening and seek to prevent the need for reactive discipline. I do, however, use restorative thinking in terms of discipline as opposed to punishment-oriented thinking.

In our schools, there can be a knee-jerk reaction to discipline issues that centers on punitive consequences. As librarians, let's push back on this practice. What can this look like in a specific moment? In my current library, we have an oddly shaped student hang-out space/conference room called The Fishbowl. This is where our large display screen/TV lives. I hadn't been at this new position long when a colleague came to me in a panic to tell me that a group of 9th graders was using the display screen to hook up their gaming console. My colleague let me know the students' names and—surprising me completely—explained that they had already emailed the principal about this breach in conduct.

The first action I took was to reply to that email explaining that no action was necessary and that I'd handle it. Next,

I connected with the students in question and we had a *conversation*. I admired their creativity and we made a plan for using the screen for gaming on a special day in the future—the last day before a break perhaps. They weren't "in trouble"—why would they be? I had never told them that the screen was off-limits. Writing this out, it still feels ridiculous. This was a group of young male students who liked to be loud with each other and who were primarily students of color. Imagine the damage that would've been done to them if they had faced some kind of consequence for engaging in a harmless, fun activity. Additionally, their relationship with the library—and with me—would have been harmed.

Restorative thinking in regards to issues of misconduct stresses repairing harm, not punishment. It involves asking questions that suspend immediate judgment. Students who have experienced the harm should have a say in how the harm is repaired, and the individuals who are responsible for causing the harm should take responsibility for repairing the harm to not just the injured party, but the school community. Restorative practices are not soft or easy. They are time-intensive and expect work and effort from the students causing harm—as opposed to punishment, which does not repair harm or restore community. Restorative justice requires administration support and whole-school training. Even though I have been trained in mediation circles, I do not have extensive personal experience in facilitating circles with injured parties—from a severe physical fight, for example. I would rely on a trained counselor or social worker to lead those circles.

Restoring and ReStorying

Amos Clifford, in *Teaching Restorative Practice with Classroom Circles*, talks about the value of circles as supporting re-storying. "Re-storying is the process by which we loosen the grip that stories that we have constructed about each other and our world have on us, thus opening up new possibilities of how we see and experience each other."[1] This describes the way in which

I've seen circles powerfully open and connect students with both each other and new ideas. For more resources on restorative practices, the below list of free resources can be a starting point.

- *Toolkit: The Foundations of Restorative Justice* from Learning for Justice (Cory Collins in Issue 66, 2021)
- *Restorative Practices: Fostering Healthy Relationships and Promoting Positive Discipline in Schools* (A Guide for Educators from the Advancement Project, 2014)
- The downloadable *Equity-Oriented Restorative Justice Resource Library* from UCLA (Anyon, Legette, Castro, Melero, Trujillo, 2022)

LEVERAGE YOUR EXPERTISE

- What decisions in your library are you already making with a restorative lens? Is there any aspect of your library program that could further benefit from a restorative mindset?
- Are there any opportunities where you could incorporate circles into your instruction?
- What are some of your favorite and proven opening questions to use with students during lessons or activities? Did you add any new ones to try from the examples in this chapter?
- Identify ways in which a restorative approach to discipline in your library has or can be implemented.

Note

1 Clifford, A. *Teaching Restorative Practice with Classroom Circles.* Center for Restorative Process, Developed for the San Francisco School District.

7

Marketing = Seeing

I often get asked by districts to "talk to my librarians about marketing their libraries." For reasons I couldn't articulate to myself, I was never as excited about this topic as other favorites, such as inclusive literature or student agency. I became much more comfortable with accepting these requests when I reframed—for both myself and librarian attendees—***marketing*** as actually ***seeing***. Seeing is twofold here: both ***seeing*** your students and ensuring that your students feel ***seen*** in and through your library program. Another way to think of this framework is through the importance of both visibility and validation. My four main touchstones for *seeing*—or visibility and validation—are knowing our students, bespoke readers' advisory, inclusive shelving and displays, and fostering a reading community.

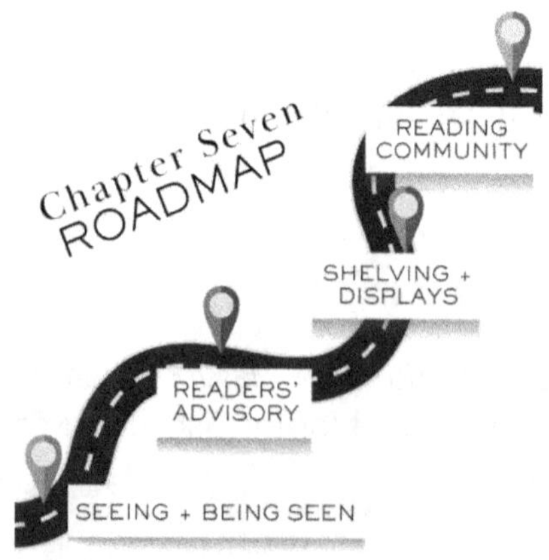

DOI: 10.4324/9781003564775-8

Knowing Your Students

Building relationships and knowing our students is at the core of what we do as school librarians. But what does "knowing our students" truly entail? I like to think of the importance of knowing my students in both micro- and macro-ways.

On a macro level, I need to have a strong grasp on what my cohorts of students are interested in—from series to games to apps to activities. What is popular right now on a general level? Additionally, what are my students encountering in the school curriculum? What are their class texts for humanities classes? On a more sensitive note, what are my students worried about? Answers to questions about class content and student anxieties can be elevated through relationships with colleagues and by embedding ourselves in team meetings and PLCs.

Macro-level data on student interests is also an essential piece. After all, not all students are comfortable enough to voice their enthusiasm and hobbies. This is where a survey can be a vital tool—but only if done intentionally and restoratively. A quick "reading survey" has the potential to turn off the very students you're attempting to reach. Instead, I frame my surveys around a wide range of student interests, not only reading.

At the beginning of each year, I create a *Fandoms and Interests Survey* to administer to students. By administer, I mean give to all students in a relaxed manner! Sometimes, I'll give the survey as part of beginning-of-year activities. I've also used class time in English classes or even used larger school "assemblies" or meetings for this purpose. On my *Fandoms and Interests Survey,* from the name to the questions, students are centered in a way that highlights that their reading experiences and tastes are not all that I'm interested in. By naming a library survey—a reading survey—we are sending the message that our interest in our students is based on if and how much they read. Which is harmful! Especially for those students who have had negative or even traumatic reading experiences in the past. *Our students don't have to earn our attention and care by being readers.* After all, I'm not interested in my students because they are readers. I'm interested in my students because they are my students. They all have rich lives, interests, and hobbies. Any surveys we give students should mirror that!

I modify my questions each year, but they follow a similar vein. Example questions include:

- What are some of your favorite things to do and/or engage with? Are you a gamer? (Which games?) Play sports? (Which ones?) You can list any activity you enjoy doing!
- Do you have a favorite series or movie? List any and all!

I also ask questions related to their library experiences and hopes or dreams for the space.

- Is there anything you wish the library had that we don't yet have?
- Is there any library reality that you would like changed this year?

The data gleaned from the survey each year is rich, and I use it to build book orders, displays, reading lists, and even programming ideas. For example, I use the series my students are most interested in each year to create engaging read-alike lists via Canva to display in the library.

Bespoke Readers' Advisory

A British word I wish would get more traction in the US is *bespoke—or custom-made, built for a specific purpose or user*. So much of my own feelings about librarianship center on building spaces and programs that are custom-made for the student(s) in front of me. *Bespoke!* Bespoke is an idea so aligned with my identity as a librarian that it's part of my social media handle. Nowhere does the "bespoke-ness" of librarianship matter more than with Readers' Advisory.

Readers' Advisory is defined differently by librarians, but at its core, it's connecting a book and its reader. This connection can even happen asynchronously through book lists and displays, but typically, we're talking about the time you spend with a patron to find the reading material they are looking for (even when, especially when, they don't know they are looking for it exactly). It's no less than a cornerstone of our work as literacy leaders and a major building block in creating a restorative library program.

Bespoke Reader's Advisory is a wheel. To do it well, we need to be learning about students—in the moment and ongoing—and when we do it well, we are constantly learning about both our students and collections. This wheel of bespoke reader's advisory is iterative, student-centered, and an investment in the literacy of our students.

We can never forget the power—and inherent responsibility—in placing a book in a student's hand. We are holding a lot in that moment that is unseen (below the iceberg). In a whirlwind of noise, students, and responsibilities, we are doing all of the below as part of our readers' advisory with students:

- Ascertaining what they are looking for—a book for pleasure reading, a class, etc.
- Assessing if they know what they may be interested in—genre or format.
- Noticing specific tastes or interests.
- Recognizing what you already **know** about a student's identity (no assumptions).
- Remembering (if possible) what the student has read before.
- Centering (pulling in from the margins) stories written by BIPOC, Queer, and/or Disabled authors in our thought process/recommendations.
- Doing all of this iteratively.

We all have our favorite prompts or structures for successful readers' advisory. Mine is a simple one: *What is the last book you remember really enjoying?* Answers are limitless to this, but fall under several major categories. How we respond to our students' answers is *just as important* as the information they give us in order to build a restorative library. Responding *without* judgment, but with a welcoming, curious, and affirming vibe, is often more important than the words we say.

STUDENT ANSWER: A specific, recent book that the student can clearly articulate.

RESPONSE: Chat about the book and make specific suggestions based on read-alikes, other titles by the same author, other titles in the same genre and/or that have the same "feel" as the book. *Novelist* is a great resource for this. Many public library systems have access to this database, so you'll be able to access it through your own login and then use it to offer suggestions, especially for books you are not familiar with. In your suggestions, make inclusive offerings. Again, inclusive books are not medicine or something to be added to a book diet. Inclusive books are food and we recommend them because yes, they represent our students and/or the global majority *and* also because they are great books.

STUDENT ANSWER: A book that the student read a while ago. For example, for HS students, we hear *Diary of a Wimpy Kid* a lot in answer to this question.

RESPONSE: Again, chat about the book as a positive literary choice. Tailor your suggestions to books you have in your collection that connect to the genre or mood of the stated title. Follow up questions can be helpful. *What was it you loved about that series?*

STUDENT ANSWER: "I don't like to read. I don't read." Or similar.

RESPONSE: "That's okay"—again, a smile. Affirm what students are telling you. I never say…"Oh, yes you do!" or "I'm sure that's not true"—restorative library interactions don't start by ignoring or arguing with what a student is sharing with you. After an "Okay!"—with a big grin, ask a follow-up question about what they like to do in their free time, in terms of activities, sports, or a favorite show or series. Validating what a student *does* like and *is* interested in goes a long way in building a positive readers' advisory experience. We can then use whatever they are interested in to find titles to recommend.

With all of these interaction examples, but especially the last two, offer this suggestion while sharing the titles: *read the first page of each and see which you like best.* We want our students to feel like they are in the driver's seat. "Come back to me if none of these work for you and we'll find something different." The subtext should be that we'll be *excited* to find something additional or different because they are such a discerning reader. Set up your students after each RA experience so that there is *no way* for them to fail. Every library interaction should be a win.

What are some of your favorite ways to open up an interaction about finding a book?

Promoting inclusive books is always the goal. Always. Holding all of this knowledge and skill set in the moment can be tricky! There are ways you can set yourself—and your readers' advisory—up for success. In addition to reading a lot yourself and keeping up-to-date with *Novelist* recommendations for popular titles in your collection, make read-alike lists so that your students can access this kind of guidance from you asynchronously, *and* you can have it for reference too! Melissa Corey has done beautiful work popularizing the display of reading lists in tabletop display flip binders and has inspired scores of librarians—including me! Some examples of lists you can create:

- Thematic: Tearjerkers, Survival Stories, Gaming, Body Horror, Sapphic Romance.
- Identity-Based for MCs: Puerto-Rican, Neurodivergent, Deaf and Hearing Impaired, Non-Binary.
- Connected to a Book Series, Game, Movie: *Adventure Time, Gilmore Girls, Arcane.*

The deeper and wider our collections of inclusive books are, the more wonderfully granular our lists can get: *Queer Thrillers that Don't Center Romance* or *Neurodivergent Fantasy*.

As you're building these lists, ensure that they are inclusive in both author identity and format. Graphic novels and manga should be on every list. Books written by BIPOC authors, Queer authors, and Disabled authors should be on every list—and all the wonderful intersections therein. If you're having trouble doing this, that's a great check that your collection needs growth. Which is okay! Think of our collections as gardens. Just as important as it is to weed, we need to be constantly planting new seeds and seedlings—and looking at new catalogs to find them. See more on inclusive literature in *Chapter 3: Curating a Restorative Collection*.

Inclusive Shelving and Displays

The perfect segue from bespoke reader's advisory is our shelving and displays. I maintain that each of our shelves is more important than any display we make. In a way, our shelves ***are*** displays—constant, visible, and ever-changing. Our libraries—every wonderful bit of them—are always talking. Always sending messages. What is *on* our shelves is covered in Chapter 3. Here, I'd like to focus on *how* we shelve; in terms of genrefication, aesthetics, and cataloguing.

Genrefication

Genrefying my fiction collection at multiple schools has been a decision I've never regretted. I think of the benefits of genrefication as the Four Is: *increase, invite, improve,* and *include.* Not only does genrefication **increase** the browsability of your collection, **invite** more student interaction, and **improve** circulation, but genrefication also provides you with a beautiful check on how your collection **includes** multiple identities at a granular level.

The first collection I genrefied was at a middle school, and I had spent years building a vibrant and inclusive collection that reflected my school community. When I genrefied, however, a glaring gap appeared: horror. (Then, as now, middle school horror is in demand. Publishers finally seem to be answering this call!) My horror section at that time, though, was overwhelmingly white and straight. This is where genrefication can be so incredibly helpful for our own collection development. It shines a light on our collection at a granular—and visible—level and provides a powerful check on the inclusivity of our collection. For my middle school horror section, I devoted resources to finding more horror with BIPOC/Queer main characters—including seeking out smaller publishers and finding "older" horror which would still work for a middle school audience.

Aesthetics

Why do aesthetics matter for a restorative library? Our libraries should be aesthetically pleasing—not in a surface-level way, but in a way that draws students into the space. For me, there is nothing so pleasing—so beautiful—as reflective book covers. My shelving and displays capitalize on covers. Face out, face out, face out! To achieve a flooding of face-out covers:

- Use every available surface for book displays. If you're like me and you've never been lucky enough to have a fancy circular display piece for books, we've learned to be creative. Use the top of bookshelves (of course), the center of tables, windowsills, and cleverly placed side tables and wall shelves to increase display square footage.

- On every shelf, devote space for face-out titles. If you have the funds for bookshelf endcap displays and modern "floating book" wall shelves, great. If not, don't despair! The book titles are what's gorgeous—not the accessories. All you need is a flat surface to get as many books as possible facing outward. It can help to stagger which side of each shelf to leave open for face out titles, to break up the eyeline and draw attention to all those covers.
- I don't make fancy displays, and please don't feel like you need to either. Our displays don't have to be Pinterest-worthy; they just need to be powerful. They need to center inclusive books in an organic way and also tie in to school activities and culture. More display ideas are in *Chapter 2: Building a Restorative Space.*

Cataloging

Implicit bias, historical racism, and heterosexism can all hide in a school library mainstay—our catalogs. How? Titles can contain tags and keywords with outdated language. Wording on classification subheadings can dehumanize. And threading through it all? A flawed system—*The Dewey Decimal Classification system*—created by, well, a flawed individual.

The Dewey Decimal system was first published in 1876, meaning that not only was the system built for a vastly different world, but its method of classification was often racist and sexist, sometimes subtly so, but often overt. Currently, books about Black history are not shelved with History in the 900s; they are under Social Sciences in the 300s. Meaning that books about President Barack Obama, would be separated from all other books on US Presidents in a school library (as of 2025). Immigrant history, women's history, and disabled history have a similar removal from the History section in Dewey. This may seem like a small issue, but it furthers the narrative that white men make history. The rest of us are addendums, located shelves away. Books centering LBGTQ+ people have undergone a long journey in Dewey. Their current spot is an improvement over past decades, but they are still found on the shelf between sex work and fetishes/BDSM and not with People.

For these reasons, many libraries are shifting away from Dewey—some are even doing away with Dewey classification for their Non-Fiction sections altogether. They are essentially "ditching Dewey" and I fall into this category myself. I have ditched Dewey at two school libraries and have never regretted it. Not only has this allowed me to work towards removing bias from our cataloguing, but it has also made our non-fiction section more intuitive and browsable. Harmful classification of our students does not fit in a restorative library.

How have I done it? First, let me be clear, I am certainly not the only one to have done this work! When I first became interested in tackling this problem in my middle school library, two wonderful Library Science students—Mara Rosenberg and Dezarae Osborne—spent the day in my non-fiction shelves, brainstorming on new sections for our collection. They were instrumental in thought-partnering with me! My middle school nonfiction collection was relatively small, and I was the only shelver. I moved my titles and made new signage, allowing students to find books easily by browsing.

At my high school, with a much larger non-fiction collection and more shelving help, I knew that I'd need to do more than reshelve the titles in a way that would make sense to me. I would need to digitally reclassify, relabel, and create a system that would make sense for shelvers, catalog searchers, *and* browsers. I toyed with using classification systems that other school librarians had developed, but I ultimately decided to just create my own that would be bespoke for both our library collection and align with our mission of equity and inclusivity.

This is a continual process. I'm two years into my new system and continue to tweak it, but it is working. Below are my current categories and subheadings, along with how I label. No numbers, simply initials. Nothing complicated. Again, this is what fits my school population and collection development goals. Maybe you have more sports books and less Dungeons and Dragons? Then, I'd break sports out into its own category and do subsections as necessary. Language continues to change. With a bespoke system, we can continue to change with it.

Category	Abbreviation
American History	AH
World History	WH
Local History + Activities	LHA
Poetry	POE
True Crime	TC
Sports + Games, Music, and Art	SAM
Being Human: Race, Gender + Sexuality	BH
Biography	BIO
Memoir + Autobiography	MEM
Plants + Animals	PA
Health, Medicine + Mental Health	HEA
Science	SCI
Philosophers, Thinkers + Essayists	PHI
Religion + Mythology	RM
Writing + Research	WR
Dungeons and Dragons	D+D

I realize that if you are part of a larger district that creates its own guidelines, this may be an initiative you can't do on your own. If so, work to remove bias as much as you can. Move books on the Civil Rights Movement to the History section. Queer books? With People in 305. Root out any biased tags and keywords when you find them in your catalog maintenance.

Fostering a Reading Community

There is no quick fix or magic bullet to building a reading community at our schools. There are, however, some foundations necessary that will make it impossible to foster a strong reading culture without them.

- A vibrant collection of fiction titles that reflect your students and their interests.
- A commitment to graphic novels and manga.
- Zero tolerance for shaming surrounding reading choices, check-out history, and lost/overdue books.

Three simple foundations. Remember, simple is not easy. To consistently embody those three foundations above? It's hard, intentional work, but, with the above, a school's reading culture *can* shift, expand, *grow*. When the foundation is already there—what else can help?

We can have success with fostering a strong reading community when we lean on three tenets: keep it invitational, welcome families, and invite all stakeholders. A main framework of my practice is that I don't force students to read. Instead, I invite them into a community of readers. It's a subtle shift in how we think about our students—and families: a community of readers. It is always, always invitational.

If you are able, consider offering an elective or club that is not only invitational, but open-ended in terms of material. At my high school, I offer an elective where every student simply… reads. Whatever they want. At the end of every term of this elective, I share student reflections—and the number of minutes spent reading—with school stakeholders, including administration and families.

Welcoming families has never been more important. Conservative groups promote a false narrative that pits families and educators against each other. We know this is not true! As librarians, we welcome family partnerships. Some of my favorite things to hear a student say are: *I'm reading this book with my mother* or *it's a read aloud for my little brother*. Families can be staunch library advocates and are especially motivated when they see their students both reading more and spending more time in our libraries. Additionally, families can be included in restorative library programs, such as #TrueBookFAIRs (see Chapter 9), school literacy nights, or community book clubs.

Including all stakeholders in fostering a reading community is key. If your school runs DEAR or SSR times, *every* staff member should be encouraged to read (and supported with reading material they are interested in): from the janitor to the principal. To help advertise the importance of reading, create signage for your staff—again, from the janitor to the math teacher to the receptionist to administration—to hang near their spaces that either shows what they are currently reading or favorite titles they've read in the past. If they don't know or are unsure, this is a great opportunity to put your amazing readers' advisory skills—and your high-interest collection—to good use with your colleagues.

LEVERAGE YOUR EXPERTISE

- What surveys have you used with students that have worked well?
- Are any sections of your library genrefied? If not, consider starting with just one part of the library, for example, graphic novels, to break out into different genres.
- Reflect on the cataloguing in your non-fiction section. Select books with LGBTQIA+ content to ensure that the keywords listed for the titles in your catalog treat the subject matter with dignity and care.
- Take a look at the current displays in your library. Are multiple identities represented? Different genres across those identities? Different formats to reflect our readers' interests?
- What community reading events have you facilitated in your library? What are you going to try next?

Seeing Our Students

When we truly see our students and ensure that they also feel seen in our spaces, we've successfully marketed our library, collection, and programs to our most important stakeholders: students. When students feel validated in our spaces, they'll help create restorative library programs in partnership with us. It's a beautiful—and powerful—cycle!

8

Restorative Clubs + Author Visits

We're often lucky enough to be the go-to person in our schools for special programming, specifically clubs and author visits. How we structure these events has a huge impact on our students' feelings of belonging in our schools. Building clubs and author visits with an equity lens can ensure that students can find a place in our libraries where they can thrive outside of academic classrooms.

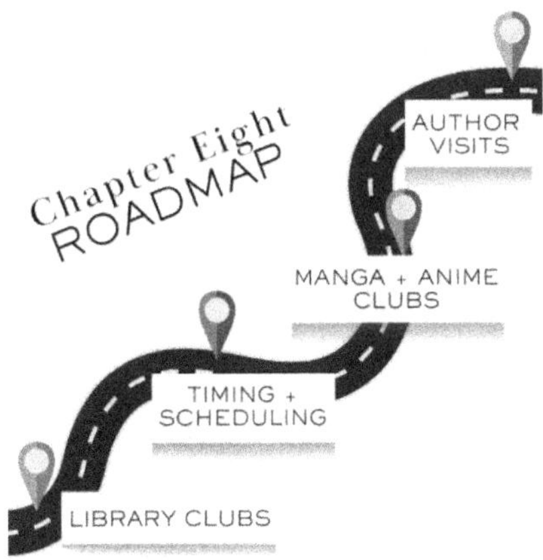

DOI: 10.4324/9781003564775-9

Clubs

When we design clubs for our libraries, we are leveraging student interests to create spaces that remove barriers and build sanctuaries. Clubs are often the physical embodiment of what makes the community-building power in libraries so vital for students. By capitalizing on our curation skills, resource knowledge, and insight into student interests, we can construct clubs where our students can both succeed and belong.

Ta-Nehisi Coates said that he was "made for the library, not the classroom. The classroom was a jail of other people's interests. The library is open, unending, free."[1] When we offer clubs that honor our students' interests—not our own—we are establishing a concrete way to ensure that our libraries can be "open, unending, and free" for our students today. When we design and facilitate clubs in a way that is truly student-centered, clubs can support social-emotional learning, student relationships, and deep interests. Additionally, clubs can cement our library as a third space—that powerful place that bridges the classroom and home. Creating spaces where students can safely celebrate their interests is essential. As librarians, it is our job to build spaces where our learners can "geek out" and wholeheartedly dive into their interests. This can be especially vital for our neurodivergent students who are often shamed for deep interests or hyper-fixations in our schools, such as a specific anime or game. Finally, to build equitable school clubs, we have to be vigilant about ensuring that we are not putting any barriers in place. All students should have access to clubs and not be limited by time, money, or transportation needs.

To build clubs to meet the largest possible range of students, it's helpful to think widely in terms of time and location. I've offered clubs during lunchtime, before and after school, during the summer, remotely, and asynchronously.

Lunchtime clubs are low-floor, high-ceiling: easy to build in terms of advertising and accessibility, but a high threshold for success and popularity. Clubs where you watch something—from anime to sports tournaments to films—are a natural fit as it's easy to eat and still fully participate. Ensure that your club is equitable for all kinds of lunch-eaters by never officially beginning the club until students who've had time to get through the lunch line are there. Otherwise, you're prioritizing students who bring their lunch to the detriment of lunch purchasers—including students receiving free or reduced cost lunches. Anime clubs are an especially well-matched fit for lunchtime clubs as the typical length of a show—less than 25 minutes—can usually still fit into a lunch period.

Due to extremely early bus routes or families with early schedules, your library may host early risers. These students may wish to be engaged with library tasks (see *Chapter 10: Library Helpers*) or use the extra time to complete classwork or read. I've had students uninterested in any of those activities, but required to be in the library per school policy. Providing appealing content in these in-between moments can sell the library even to students who might not have ever chosen to be there. Depending on the ages of your students and your school's phone policies, you may also be motivated to steer students to non-screen activities. I've used this time to build casual, unstructured clubs around interests I've gently "pulled" out of these early-in-the-day visitors. Student favorites have included puzzles, card games, and board games. I've written Donors Choose grants—with these early risers—to select engaging supplies for the library. My students recommend you get *UNO* (with a shout-out for *GIANT UNO*), *Jenga* (play on a mat to reduce the noise), *Code Names, Pokémon* puzzles, *Taco Cat Goat Cheese Pizza*, and *Spot It!* These suggestions can be adapted for different age levels.

I only recommend running *structured* after-school clubs if there is transportation provided or available. Otherwise, you're preventing full access for students and sorting potential participants based on who has families with flexible schedules and access to a car. If you are in a neighborhood school where walking is possible for everyone or in an urban school with reliable public transportation, that gives you more potential for running after school clubs. Otherwise, you either have to find school funds for transportation or coordinate with other bus routes—with athletics, for example. Only after you ensure that not having "a way home" won't preclude participation, the sky is the limit for what you can offer, or more restoratively, what you can *create* with students.

Our favorite after school club at Mount Vernon? It was our *Tristan Strong* Book Club. I was able to offer this club because our school had used funds to provide busing and snacks for after school enrichment. There was already a plethora of sports and creative clubs offered, and students asked for something different. I had just read *Tristan Strong Punches a Hole in the Sky* by Kwame Mbalia (Rick Riordan Presents, 2019) and loved that it was suspenseful, humorous, mythology- and folklore-rich, and featured a main character who shared key identity points with so many of my students. I shared the book with students, and they immediately wanted to create a book club and invite local author Mr. Mbalia for a visit. Students co-facilitated our sessions and we read, listened to the audiobook, designed sneakers for each character, wrote poetry, and had character debates.

In our schools, there are (often) oddly named times where you have opportunities to build something with and for students. At Mount Vernon, it was MAV time. At my son's school with a plane for a mascot, it was Flight School. School with a dolphin mascot? Free Swim. You get the idea! Using those times for activities and ad-hoc clubs is a great opportunity to connect with more students. Query students for interests and create away. I've done a truly eclectic assortment of programming, including: News Show clubs, Calligraphy, Best Basketball Plays (watching and discussing top 10 ankle breakers, slams, etc.), Japanese and Korean (using free language learning sites through the public library with native Japanese and Korean speakers), Chopped cooking competitions, Sphero, manga, anime art, bullet journaling, graffiti art, and horror movie making.

An asynchronous club might sound like an oxymoron, but I've had success with building a large 3D printing club this way. There are some students who are not able to access the kinds of "free" periods I'm describing in the above paragraph due to absences or the need for remediation or make-up work during "free time" in the school day. Every student deserves access to library clubs! To build my (asynchronous) 3D Printing Club,

I created a class through Tinkercad (tinkercad.com) and a short training video for students to access on their own in the library. (The training video consisted of some basic 3D printing vocabulary, safety reminders, and examples of meaningful 3D printed projects.) From there, students start progressing through tutorials on Tinkercad. All of this can be done in five to ten minute chunks so students can access this club at various times in the school day (or even at home). When students are ready to print their own design—or one they've found on a creation site like Thingiverse (thingiverse.com)—we schedule a time to begin. Even though students are rarely working with each other in the same time and place, there is still shared excitement around classmates' builds.

In March of 2020, my lunchtime anime clubs came to an abrupt halt when school was disrupted by Covid-19. After devices and necessary hotspots were delivered in our district, I immediately began offering remote clubs to continue our lunchtime series. In those first few months of remote instruction, these anime clubs were a constant for my students in what felt like a very unstable social landscape. I kept my remote clubs running throughout that first summer and the next school year. Even when we returned to in-person schooling full-time, our remote clubs lived on. The freedom and flexibility of remote clubs meant that I was not bound by space or school.

I continued to run both middle-school and high-school remote clubs that included current students, former students, friends of students at other schools, and other teens in my district who I'd adopted into my clubs. I never required cameras—in fact, we would often communicate with each other about and through our PFPs (profile pictures) we used on our Google Meets. Additionally, posting in the chat while we were watching shows added a layer to our community that was a perfect fit: easy, low-risk communication. For students who struggle with communication, this feature helped increase their confidence in social situations. During one club, a club member (who was a friend of a former student) said in the chat: *This club literally saved my year, TBH.* As a librarian, what more could we ask for? Remote clubs benefit from a Learning Management System. I used Google Classroom, (but any LMS will work), and created separate classrooms for each club. If you open the chat in your LMS to students, make sure to participate and monitor to sustain a safe online community.

I cannot stress enough how important manga and anime clubs are. As a librarian, I see my role as three-fold: nurturing my students' reading lives, their interests, and their whole, full selves in and through a library which serves as an incubator of joy and belonging. Nowhere does this live out more powerfully—and connect with all three tenets—than with manga and anime clubs. Manga readers and anime watchers are overrepresented in marginalized communities, including Black youth, Latinx youth, Queer, and Neurodivergent youth—and all the intersectionalities therein.[2] Creating safe spaces for these students amidst the hate and vitriol their communities are experiencing is essential. A manga or anime club can be a sanctuary. There are student comments about our manga and anime clubs that showcase their importance.

- When there is a common interest, we just click together.
- I feel safer here than anywhere else.
- Even in a remote environment, you can get close to people fast.
- There is just so much to talk about; all the time.
- I know I'm not going to be shamed for what I like when I'm in club.

A quick note on building clubs which respond to and reflect student interests. There will be times when you are not equipped–culturally or experience-wise—to successfully facilitate a club on your own. For example, you may have students who want to learn how to step—a dance and movement that is a historical form of storytelling typically performed by Divine Nine Black Sororities and Fraternities. If you are not a member of a Divine Nine Sorority or Fraternity, honor the historical roots of this art form by reaching out to Divine Nine members on your teaching staff or active groups and alumni in your area.[3] Just as you would ask for visiting experts on a subject matter you need guidance on, rely on cultural experts as well.

Author Visits

Author visits honor the people crafting the powerful stories we read and can generate interest around literacy and books amongst students. However, they have an overwhelming potential to be inequitable in both construction and execution. First, we must be intentional about who we invite to our school. For all the same reasons we collect and use reflective, inclusive literature, we need to be bringing authors and artists to our schools who reflect our students' identities, languages, and lived experiences. Additionally, once authors are at our schools, their time should be allocated in equitable ways for our students. Face time with authors should not be given only to students who purchase books to gain entrance to a book signing line. We don't want to sort students for activities on the basis of finances.

With elementary librarians Liz Porter and Kathryn Cole and UNC School of Information and Library Science Professor Sandra Hughes-Hassell, we developed an equitable author visit model. After hosting authors in our schools for residences, visits, and zoom calls, we developed a list of best practices to keep author visits both equity-framed and student-centered. We identified six necessary touchstones to build author and/or writing experiences within an equity framework. Based on our experiences, we suggest that author visits should:

1. Build a learning environment that honors and amplifies student voice.
2. Collaborate with stakeholders to ensure the program resonates, fostering engagement for reading in the classroom and beyond.
3. Select students with a framework that strives to eliminate sorting based on systemic, racially oppressive factors such as behavior or reading levels, and prioritizes students for any chosen workshops from traditionally marginalized communities.
4. Foreground culturally-sustaining instructional strategies.

5. Reaffirm positive racial/ethnic identity and infuse the entire process with joy.
6. Remove grading or high-pressure assignments. Focus is on welcoming and appreciating authentic voices and workshopping with students.

We've used this same model for countless author and writing experiences, including virtual visits. When we bring artists and authors to connect with our students, we must be intentional at every step, from choosing the writer to organizing the content and activities. Often, there is a notion of "how these things are done" or "this is what people are used to," and this results in a large assembly of a librarian's favorite author and a money-necessary signing line. This can reinforce systems that deny opportunities to students from economically-disadvantaged backgrounds and/or marginalized communities. Instead, we can shift our thinking and help shift the thinking of stakeholders in our schools and create author experiences that are more empowering—complete with authors who reflect our students and meaningful writing activities that center our students.

LEVERAGE YOUR EXPERTISE

- When you think about your most successful clubs, what attributes did they share?
- What has been your most popular time for offering clubs? Is there a part of the school day that might work for additional club programming?
- What barriers can you identify that may keep students from being able to participate in your library's clubs?
- When you reflect on author visits, how well have visiting authors reflected your students' lived experiences?

Belonging

What we call our clubs or experiences doesn't matter nearly as much as how they are impacting our students. All of our programming—no matter how we refer to it—should help our students feel like they belong in our libraries and at our schools. For me, there is no more magical or restorative moment in our libraries than when students are safely, animatedly, and joyously engaged with each other around a shared interest. It feels like a sanctuary. It feels like *belonging*.

Notes

1 Coates, T. (2015). *Between the World and Me.* Text Publishing Company, Melbourne, VIC, Australia.
2 Hawkins, A., Ratica, E., Smith, S., Stivers, J., and Touré, S. (2025). *Manga Goes to School.* Chicago, IL: ALA Editions.
3 I actually did pledge a Divine Nine Sorority in college—***Delta Sigma Theta***—AND as a white librarian, I would not co-opt a culture that is not my own to teach students how to step.

9

#TrueBookFAIRs

One of the most harmful—and non-restorative—practices in school libraries are traditional book fairs. Surprised? I know that they are well-loved by many, but consider the traditional book fair model. Libraries are turned into for-profit satellite shops for publishers, where students and families have to buy access to its resources. Students are sorted—sometimes even literally—into who can afford to purchase items at the fair and who cannot. Many economically marginalized parents have identified book fairs as among the "most embarrassing" events at their children's schools.[1] As librarians, we should be careful not to embrace events that may embarrass or humiliate families. In many cases, schools close libraries during book fairs, potentially cutting off access to books for students who can't afford to purchase books while expanding access to students who *can* afford to do so.

Are there any positive outcomes to book fairs that we can save? Of course. Book fairs can generate excitement for reading and literacy. They can offer a pathway for book ownership of self-selected titles. They also champion reading for pleasure. Can we create programs that accomplish all of these positive outcomes while preventing inequitable sorting by excluding students and families? *Yes*. Yes, if we bravely reimagine the school book fair to be something different. At #TrueBookFAIRs, students select new books to keep from a fair collection of all new books that have

DOI: 10.4324/9781003564775-10

been intentionally and lovingly curated to reflect students and their interests. There is no cost to students. Ever.

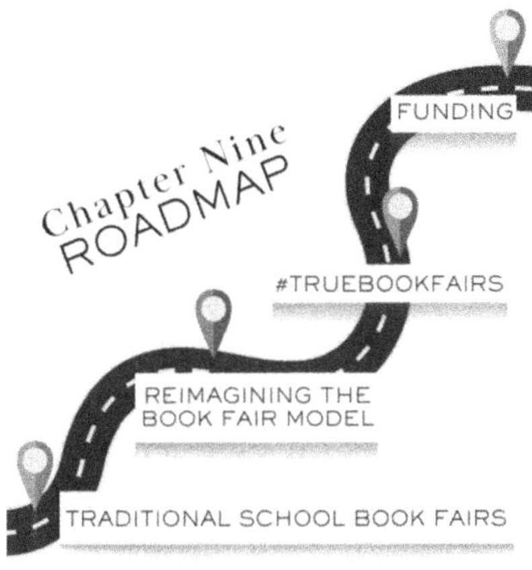

The First #TrueBookFAIR

One of the first questions that teachers asked me when I began at Mount Vernon in my first year as a librarian was: *Are you going to have a Book Fair?* Internally, I was screaming "NO," but offered a non-committal "*we'll see*" in those first few months. (I hadn't learned how to say no to adults yet.) I knew that I would never run a traditional book fair. When I had volunteered at my children's elementary school book fairs, I watched with horror at how students were *sorted*. I'm using the word *sorted* intentionally. For some classes, students who did not have money to shop at the fair sat on the floor in a row while their classmates with money shopped at the fair. From that moment on, I was soured on the entire book fair concept. As I studied to become a librarian and learned more about systemic oppression in education, I wondered how we could do something different; how we could mitigate the embarrassment, the unfairness, the inequity. As a profession, we can be suspicious when people tell us—*well, this is the way it's always been done.* I dislike the traditional book fair model for every school, but especially schools with a large percentage of economically disadvantaged families, as evidenced by the number of students receiving free and reduced lunches. My school—where I was being asked to run a book fair—was such a school. Internally, I was still screaming.

I was also scheming. Our school's social worker—who was the Family Engagement Chair—shared with staff that there were funds in the Title 1 budget earmarked for family events to spend before the end of the year. I immediately said: *I have a family event idea!* I pitched a May free book fair that would be open to students and families, championing literacy across all ages. Probably due to the passion I had for the idea, the administration signed on. My plan was simple—create my own fair, where no money would be allowed in the door. Students and families could come and "shop" for books.

To make my plans financially feasible, I chose a publisher's warehouse sale as my primary source of materials. I wanted to elicit buy-in from students before the event, so I went to them for book suggestions, from specific titles to most wanted genres and formats. The conversations during those planning sessions were enlightening. Many students told me that they had both loved and hated book fairs at their previous schools. They loved seeing all the new books, but hated that they were not able to buy anything. One of my students, Zach, summed it up perfectly: "Seriously. They were Book UNFairs. You are having an actual BookFAIR." The #TrueBookFAIR was born.

In keeping with my inclusive book collecting ethos, I purchased books for the fair that were reflective of my students, their experiences, and their interests. I was a smart shopper, both financially and from an equity perspective. I bought mostly middle-grade and young adult titles. To celebrate family reading, I also purchased picture books, board books, and early chapter books for younger siblings and cousins. I purchased over 400 titles for our school. I structured our family event to look like a typical book fair with signage, displays, and genre groupings. Bilingual students helped me create signs in Spanish.

That first #TrueBookFAIR family night was a powerful literacy experience. Students were engaged and excited to select books. They were also a bit disbelieving. "I can pick whichever book I want?""I can just leave with it?""I can get one, and my sister can get one?" Yes. Yes. *Yes*. Families were excited as well, not only with the book fair, but with seeing the library and how it was designed to welcome and include their children.

Even though the original event was built through Family Engagement funds, I knew I didn't want to deny access to students who were unable to make our Family Night. After all, we cannot punish students who are unable to attend nighttime events. Not only is it typically out of students' control, it disproportionately affects families who are not working 9-to-5 jobs and who have transportation or childcare challenges. (A key tenet of restorative family events in the library—or anywhere—is to be clear that all ages are welcome!) To include all students in this new book fair, I also scheduled Language Arts classes to visit in the days following our family night, so every student could "shop" the fair during the school day. With a typical book fair, this is a complicated multi-day process where students fill out a wish list, complete with prices, to bring home to families. They are then supposed to bring money on another day for the actual purchasing.

With a #TrueBookFAIR, this process is all simplified. Students come. They see a book they like. They leave with it. They own it. That first fair taught me that self-selection + ownership + reflective, inclusive books = literacy magic. Money should have no part in this equation for our students.

#TrueBookFAIRs Every Year: Well, More Than Once a Year

#TrueBookFAIRs became a foundational part of my library program at Mount Vernon. I held two each year—one in the fall or winter and one in May. Each one I organized and experienced strengthened my belief in its framework. After over 15 fairs, the premise has stayed the same: students select new books to keep from a fair collection that I have intentionally and lovingly curated to reflect our students and their interests. There is no cost to students. Additionally, #TrueBookFAIRs are never framed in charity. They are not situated as a freebie that was given to my students because they may come from low-income families. They are, as I tell students, simply *how we do things in this library*.

Oh, and in terms of library access? I never close the library for check-outs during a #TrueBookFAIR.

When we curate collections with entire families in mind, we support whole-family literacy. At subsequent family nights, I built stations for younger family members to engage with (coloring, blocks, etc.) and included picture book read-alouds. Each school-day fair would also include a picture book/board book collection for students to pick out for younger family members. Hearing students talk about which book they were going to gift and read to which family member was both heartwarming and powerful.

Let's Talk About the Money

I live in the real world with you. We know that as school librarians, we are constantly fighting for robust budgets for our libraries. I also understand that for some, profits from book fairs fill your shelves. That's another problem! We shouldn't be relying on financial support from families to build our collections. All school libraries need administrative and financial support to build inclusive collections. Book fair profits should not be a foundational collection development strategy.

The number one question I get is *where do you get the money*? Through different years, I've funded fairs in a combination of ways. The constants are starting with a small fund of money from administration—usually from Title 1 funds—and then supplementing with donations of new books, ARCs from authors and publishers, and free books from conferences. It is a year-long hustle. I am always looking for *new* books! I purchase books from First Book and the Scholastic Warehouse sales. First Book's Book Bank offerings are especially helpful! During remote learning in 2020, DonorsChoose supported a remote fair. Once you start running a different sort of fair, you'll be surprised at how many people offer you books! I always keep my core tenets in mind. We should only include new books in our fair collections that our students want. If people donate books to me that I do not feel are a good fit for our book fair collection, I say thank you and turn around and donate them somewhere else. #TrueBookFAIRs are not charity. They are school library-sponsored programs to support reading for pleasure.

I piloted this program at a small school. Still, most of my fairs had over 900 books available. If I was at a larger school, I would simply start with one grade and support the same grade each year to reach a different cohort of students. If I was at a larger school, I would also have more storage room and would work to slowly build my ongoing fair collection so I could have even more titles. At Mount Vernon, I was in a tiny library in terms of space, and I made it work. A reimagined book fair is possible at any-sized school!

Wonderfully, many other librarians at other schools have worked to bring the #TrueBookFAIR model to their schools. I'm inspired by how they adapt the model, improve upon it, and make it their own!

- Kathryn Cole, a K-5 Librarian at Northside Elementary School in Chapel Hill, NC is supported by her local Public School Foundation.
- Chris Tuttell, a 9-12 Librarian at South Garner High School in Garner, NC runs #TrueBookFAIRs with Title 1 funds and donations.
- Maura Madigan, prek-5 Librarian at North Springfield Elementary School in Springfield, VA runs #TrueBookFAIRs with DonorsChoose grants, Lisa Libraries grant, and a PTA-sponsored Amazon wish list.
- Jenni Clark, K-5 Librarian at Ben Martin Elementary in Fayetteville, NC relies on community partnerships and donations and collected over 4000 books for her first free fair.

#TrueBookFAIRs Forever: Whatever They Are Called

At my current school I knew I wanted to run a reimagined book fair my very first year. I decided to brand it as a Pop-Up Book Shop. Its core tenets were the same: students could choose new books to keep from an inclusive collection I had intentionally and lovingly curated to reflect their interests. Again, there was no cost for students. As I was now at a high school, I curated YA and adult books. I relied again on ARCs, conference freebies, donations, and new books thrifted from local shops. Instead of having students visit through Language Arts classes, I went through Advisory (homeroom) groups to organize student customers for the fair. Similar to Mount Vernon, students were surprised, engaged, and excited. Most importantly, *they were reading*. I've been at two very different schools and have used the same book fair model.

LEVERAGE YOUR EXPERTISE

- Reflect on past book fair experiences at your school. What have been the highlights? What would you change?
- Imagine a book fair outcome that would be restorative for your students—all your students. What would you need to do to make that outcome a reality?
- To help in building a restorative book fair model for your school, what allies in your school, district, or community can you identify?
- What funding avenues are possible resources for you? Title 1 funds, community partnerships, corporate sponsors, donations, PTA support, grants, school budgets?

You know your school better than anyone else! Access, equitable literacy, humiliation-free book fairs, and a flood of new books are the goal. Perhaps there is a part of my model which may work at your school. You can always start small and grow each year. At their core, libraries should be for everyone, all the time. When we challenge the traditional book fair model and create something more equitable, we are restoring our libraries to be truly free and accessible. We can transform school book fairs together!

Note

1 Gorski, P. (2022). "Stop Punishing Poverty in Schools." *ASCD*, December 1, 2022.

10

Library Helpers: Beyond the Clerical

Having helpers in the library is not a new idea! Across grades and schools, many libraries have students who assist the library in some capacity. They may be called media assistants, teacher assistants, or media helpers. They may come before school, during a club, or even as part of a secondary class. Often, these helpers are given clerical tasks, from checking in and shelving books to processing and labeling new titles. With the defunding of many professional library assistant positions, this assistance from our students can be life-saving! Additionally, integrating students into the administration of the library program is a boon for building relationships and embedding the library into the culture of the school.

Moving beyond the clerical, however, can help truly build a restorative library program. Having students design signage and bookmarks, build displays, and drive library activities showcases student voice and improves the inclusivity of the library. Furthermore, when your library helpers reflect your school community across identities, your library—as the literacy center of the school—will more accurately mirror your students as a whole.

DOI: 10.4324/9781003564775-11

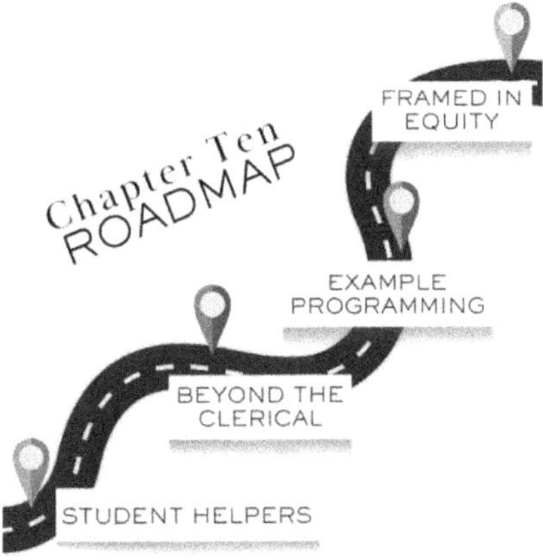

Getting Started

When I was a middle school librarian, I worked on both clerical and creative tasks with students. At the time, I thought I really had the whole library helper thing down pat. Fast forward to my first year in my current role: a librarian for Grades 9 through 12 at an independent school where students are required to earn extensive service credits as a graduation component. One of the ways in which students can earn service credits is to be a Teacher Assistant—or TA—for a staff member. The librarian who was in my role before me told me to accept one or two TAs *at most* and offered specific names of students with library experience for whom I should accept. You can probably guess—at this stage in the book—that I did not take that advice! As student after student came to me to ask if they could be my TA, I realized that here was an amazing opportunity for me as a new staff member to set an inclusive, open tone for library programming.

In my first term, I had 12 TAs. My second, 17, and by my third term, I had 19 TAs spread over eight class times. I said yes to everyone who asked me. (Generally speaking, I really try to say *yes* to students in the library as much as I can.) In the beginning of that first year, I was weeding and adding so many titles that the extra processing help was appreciated. As the months passed, however, and my number of TAs continued to grow, I knew that I was going to have to expand my thinking about what my student helpers and I could do together.

During trial and error that first year, I built a TA program that strove to move beyond the clerical and even beyond the creative. I had to provide meaningful activities for 19 students in 70-minute chunks, in addition to doing all the things we do as librarians each day. In *Core Values in School Librarianship: Responding with Commitment and Courage*, school librarians Meg Boisseau Allison and Peter Patrick Langella define inclusion as "welcoming and affirming the voices of all library stakeholders in a way that shares power."[1] I would not have been sharing power in our library if I had not said *yes* to every potential TA. The status quo was to include those with library experience, who, before I came, had been two white female students who read voraciously and were frequent library users. My first term TAs that had asked to help in the library included non-female students, BIPOC students, students who did not identify as readers, and students who were not frequent library users. Why did so many students ask me? Because I was someone new? Because I have a welcoming vibe? My transparency about the library being a soft place to land? Who knows?! *It doesn't matter.* What mattered in each of those moments was me simply saying *yes*. I've found—across all aspects of librarianship—what matters is often saying *yes* to students.

The Nuts and Bolts

So what did my TAs and I do together that first year and beyond? Well, first, we read. As student after student asked to be a TA, I realized that this would also be an avenue to highlight books in the collection through students visibly reading in the library throughout the school day. Before I came, the library primarily served as a study and classwork space, and I wanted to change the culture to highlight the power of choice-based reading. For each of my TAs, we did an individualized Reader's Advisory connection to ensure that everyone had a book to read for at least part of every TA period. For students who were not accustomed to reading in sustained blocks, we built up our time slowly, and I would also join to read with them in proximity—and community—when able. In addition to our literacy baseline, below are additional projects my TAs and I envisioned and enacted for our shared space.

- **Library Murals.** Art on our library walls is a perfect opportunity to showcase student talent, bring color to our spaces, and reflect student interests! I have a wall of manga characters that Sol designed and continues to embellish. We have a panel of scenes ripped from books that Alex created to showcase titles across text, manga, and graphic novel formats: *Lord of the Rings*, *g i v e n*, and *The Tea Dragon Society*. These murals inspire both artists and readers, highlight books across the collection, and add a WOW factor for all stakeholders.
- **Comic Pages**. For a professional project I was working on, there was a need for a student artist to illustrate a librarian's manga story. After working with Alex on this project, I realized that the possibilities for the library were endless! I guarantee that you have aspiring comic artists in your school. Tap into their talent by inviting them to create for your library! Instead of a sign instructing students how to self-checkout, display panels created by your students *showing* the check-out process. Your students can create panels detailing library procedures, community norms, fun facts, anything!
- **Read-Alike Lists**. We're all familiar with read-alike lists to connect students to books in our collection that connect to popular films, series, and other titles. Typically, these are current series or new Netflix adaptations. One day, Neema said to me: "We really need a *Gilmore Girls* one!" I hadn't considered using "older" series until that moment! Using student survey data, my students embarked on an in-depth dive into building read-alike lists for shows (both old and new, but mostly older), specifically popular with our students—from *All-American*

to *Gilmore Girls* to *House*. I scaffolded this project for my TAs so that they followed a set path to research and discover key themes or adjectives to describe the core series, new books to purchase, and finally created the signage for our library and website.

- **Manga Signage**. As stated before, manga is necessary for an equity-driven library! To highlight the beauty of the collection and improve browsability, I wanted to physically—and artistically—separate the series. Attached to unused magazine holders, Leigha created watercolor signs highlighting the series' title art to be placed on the shelf between series. You could have student helpers create signage across the library, prioritizing the series students most connect with.
- **Ordering Consultations**. Collection development must include our students—always. We should be gathering suggestions for book purchases and learning about our students so we can reflect their identities, lived experiences, and interests in our collections. Django Paris said, "Think of your syllabus as an act of resistance; something to be posted in the streets, handed out at rallies."[2] As librarians, this is how we should think of our order lists! As acts of resistance to beautifully show the identities our students inhabit and the real histories our communities have experienced and forged. We should be proud to share our draft order lists with students and excited about gathering their feedback. Having students assist with this effort is an excellent way to share power!
- **Adopt-a-Shelf**. I used this activity frequently in my middle school library as it's a wonderful way to have student helpers who perhaps only have five minutes to help at a time! Invite students to adopt a shelf—especially in their favorite format and/or genre—and those students will assume 'ownership' over its upkeep and titles on display. Additionally, students can suggest titles specific to their adopted shelves.
- **3D Printing Library Fidgets and Display Stands**. Part of a restorative helper program in our libraries is

broadening the way we think about library helpers. Expanding beyond set times…and even set spaces. Several of my library "helpers" assist me even though they do their "work" outside of the library—designing and then printing fidgets and display stands to use in the library space. If you have a 3D printer in your space, these projects can be seamlessly absorbed into your programming. If, however, your school has a 3D printer but it lives in another space, having students willing to assist you is a great way to approach students who may or may not already be frequent library visitors. Additionally, by printing fidgets to have readily available to lend and give, you'll be supporting the SEL of students and cementing the library as a welcoming place for every type of learner.
- **Weeding Class Book Sets**. Does your school have a room or closet where class book sets are kept? A graveyard of sorts of dated series, forgotten titles, and (perhaps) hidden gems? I had a small group of TAs who were objectively thrilled to have the freedom to organize the school's book room. While identifying and sorting the titles, I encouraged my students to ask themselves these questions as they were discovering class texts: *What do I notice? What do I wonder? Whose stories do I see? Whose stories are missing?* As I check in with this small crew as they continue to work on this project, we've had rich conversations about representation, the value (or not) of "classics," and who has the power to choose what we read. This project is ongoing, but will culminate with a suggested list of titles to weed that we will bring to the ELA department. Having your library helpers assist in the working of the English department highlights the library as a hub of literacy for the entire school. A project such as this also includes and educates students in deselection decision-making and inclusive curation.

My students are amazing. *Your* students are amazing! Meaningfully integrating library helpers into your library will result in a more inclusive and restorative program, increased student reading time, more opportunities for collaboration with school staff, a colorful, appealing space, and, most importantly, another pathway to cultivate and highlight student brilliance.

The Bottom Line

A group of my library helpers and I recently presented our experiences at our state library conference to a room of elementary, middle, and high school librarians. My recent presentations (and historically all my presentations) at this conference had been explicitly equity-centered including sessions on Queer literature, equitable literacy instruction with graphic novels, and culturally responsive librarianship. I made it clear that this topic—*Expanding the Role of the "Library Helper"*—was no less important for an inclusive library. Issues of equity in school librarianship are not something to be sprinkled on the top of our practice. They instead must be the foundation for all we do, including, yes, how we welcome and support assistance in the library. If you're still not sold on how library helpers support an equity-centered library, consider these components.

- Our helpers should authentically reflect our student population. If they don't, this is cause for reflection on our part. *How can I ensure that my library is seen as welcoming to all of my students? How can I ensure that I am approachable? How is my library communicating that it is owned by all?*
- Our helpers should include students who don't (yet) identify as readers. It's important for my students to know that I'm not interested in them because they are readers. I'm interested in them—all of them—because they are my students. Having self-proclaimed non-readers as library assistants is hugely important to spread (and demonstrate) this message.
- Our students shouldn't be limited by time or space. Perhaps there is a student who could be integrated into your library programming, but they don't have time in their schedule. Be open to a myriad of structures to welcome students' talents. Additionally, don't limit students

by perceived "behavior" issues. Being included in our library programs is a right, *not* a privilege to be earned by arbitrary standards of behavior codes that are historically rooted in racial bias.

- Our students should feel supported by a flexible, nurturing educator who has high expectations for them. After my first term in my new school, our Learning Specialist started referring students who had multiple learning accommodations to fulfill their TA service requirement with me. She knows that, yes, I'm a soft place to land for students throughout the day. I listen. I'm flexible. I'm understanding. She also knows that I have high expectations for all of my students. I'm nurturing, *and* I have high expectations for what students can do and discover. Both of these realities can be true.

A restorative library is built on the core values of joy and belonging. Establishing an inclusive library helper program that both celebrates and humanizes our students is an essential, restorative piece.

LEVERAGE YOUR EXPERTISE

If you currently have a library helper program:

- Reflect on your current program. What are its strengths and most meaningful aspects?
- Identify at least one creative programming idea from the chapter to introduce or adapt for your library.
- When you think of your library helpers, do they reflect your school community as a whole?

If you do not have a library helper program:

- Identify ways that you can invite students to help with the running of the library. You can start "small" with art, adopt-a-shelf, or display consultations.

Notes

1 Moreillon, J. (2021). *Core Values in School Librarianship: Responding with Commitment and Courage.* Santa Barbara, CA: Libraries Unlimited.
2 Paris, D. (2018). *International Literacy Association Keynote.* Austin, TX, July 2018.

For Product Safety Concerns and Information please contact our EU representative GPSR@taylorandfrancis.com
Taylor & Francis Verlag GmbH, Kaufingerstraße 24, 80331 München, Germany

www.ingramcontent.com/pod-product-compliance
Lightning Source LLC
LaVergne TN
LVHW010840120826
845149LV00017B/3321

* 9 7 8 1 0 3 2 8 7 1 1 8 9 *